Dwarf Hamsters as Pets.

Dwarf Hamsters book for care, costs, feeding, housing and health.

By

Jonathan Beverley

ALL RIGHTS RESERVED. This book contains material protected under International and Federal Copyright Laws and Treaties.

Any unauthorized reprint or use of this material is strictly prohibited. No part of this book may be reproduced or transmitted in any form or by any means, electronic, mechanical or otherwise, including photocopying or recording, or by any information storage and retrieval system without express written permission from the author.

Copyright © 2017

Published by: Zoodoo Publishing

Table of Contents

Table of Contents 3

Introduction 4

Chapter 1: About Dwarf Hamsters 8

Chapter 2: Deciding on a Dwarf Hamster as a Pet 15

Chapter 3: Cost of Keeping a Dwarf Hamster 33

Chapter 4: Creating a Healthy Living Environment 38

Chapter 5: Day-to-Day Care of your Dwarf Hamster 53

Chapter 6: Dwarf Hamster Body Language 64

Chapter 7: Dwarf Hamster Fighting 67

Chapter 8: Health and Veterinary Care 70

Chapter 9: Breeding Dwarf Hamsters 105

Chapter 10: Further Online Reading 114

Introduction

This book is written by a genuine animal lover for other small animal lovers who want to educate themselves on dwarf hamsters in captivity as pets and how to care for them. It is not written for readers looking for scientific facts or readers who are already experts in the field of dwarf hamster care in captivity, and are seeking deeper knowledge on these tiny rodents.

Dwarf hamsters are cute, tiny rodents that have only recently become popular with small pet owners and differ from the more common Syrian hamster because of their small size. On average, Syrian hamsters measure around 15 centimetres or 6 inches in comparison to the 9 centimetres or 4 inches of dwarf hamsters.

Dwarf hamsters first appeared on the domestic small pet scene sometime around the early 1970's but were not common-place and had to be obtained from breeders. They appeared in the commercial pet trade on a large scale in the mid-1990's and have since grown in popularity with small pet owners.

Unfortunately, as with anything that gains popular traction with the buying public - animal or otherwise, unscrupulous traders quickly recognise a source of profit and dwarf hamsters have not escaped this unwanted attention. Inter-breeding, cross-breeding and what has been termed "cruel breeding" has led to many variations in colour, size and temperament. This type of breeding means that buyers cannot always be assured that they are buying a healthy animal and could encounter problems with the animals' predictive behaviour, health, lifespan and genetic defects.

In typical hamster fashion, dwarf hamsters store food in their cheek pouches, which not only makes them look extremely cute, but can also give the impression that they are bigger than what they really are.

In the wild they live in groups and thrive in forests, grasslands and deserts of China, Kazakhstan, Mongolia and Siberia. Biologists recognise three different types of dwarf hamster species, including Russian Winter White, Campbell's and Roborovski. Since becoming popular as pets, there are many hybrid forms on the market as a result of breeding between the species.

Dwarf hamsters are predominantly nocturnal and spend most of the day sleeping. From early evening and throughout the night they are very active and in the wild they would spend their night foraging for food, digging burrows and storing food. Although territorial, they keep very busy and a healthy dwarf hamster can run up to 160 kilometres or 100 miles around their territory in one night. This means that you have to provide your pet dwarf hamster with a cage that allows enough running space, including tunnels, at least one exercise wheel and other interesting obstacles and features to keep them busy and entertained.

Dwarf hamsters can make excellent household pets for adults and late-teens, but their care must never be left entirely in the hands of even an older child; adult supervision of the care of these small fragile animals is essential.

Never acquire a dwarf hamster (or any type of pet) on impulse, give any pet as a gift or buy a pet because it looks cute. All pets are living, sentient beings that require daily care, attention and commitment for the entire duration of their natural life and in the case of dwarf hamsters, that can be for up to four years.

Before you buy a dwarf hamster it is essential that you conduct extensive research into their behaviour, cost and time investment required to ensure that they suit your budget and lifestyle. Keeping dwarf hamsters (as with any type of pet) costs money to feed, maintain and take proper care of them. Neglect leads to illness, pain, suffering and even death, and dwarf hamsters are very fragile little animals. If you are not willing to make the commitment of time and money to give your dwarf hamster a good and happy life, don't get one!

If you are willing to invest in owning a dwarf hamster you will be rewarded with hours of entertainment watching these busy little animals going about their feeding, exercise and regular routines. Most enjoy human contact and you can interact and play with them. Because of their small size, care must be exercised when handling and playing with them to avoid injuring them, or unintentionally allowing them to escape.

There are publications that teach you how to train dwarf hamsters to do tricks, and others that give ideas for dwarf hamster clothing. Dwarf hamsters are for the most part still wild little animals that have been introduced to the pet trade in the last few decades. As an animal lover and the author of this book, I am not in favour of coercing any animal into performing tricks purely for human entertainment and much prefer to let the animal behave in a manner true to its own personality. Coercing any animal to perform tricks involves a certain degree of discipline; not healthy 'behave well' discipline, but punishment versus reward discipline, and in my opinion such unhealthy pressure on any animal is unjustified! I am also against dressing a dwarf hamster in clothing. It is totally unnatural, can cause the dwarf hamster physical injury, trauma and if bits of clothing are ingested it could lead to the dwarf hamster's death. Don't put clothing on a dwarf hamster; it isn't cute, it's cruel!

It is important to note that owning hamsters of any species is illegal in Hawaii and Australia.

There is very little regulation or legislation on ownership or breeding of dwarf hamsters in most other countries around the world, and although hybrid breeding has become considered torture-breeding (which covers the illegal breeding of all animals, reptiles and birds) and is forbidden by law in several European countries, including Germany and Austria - very little is actually done with regards to policing, investigating and convicting anyone guilty of these unethical practices and en-mass breeding thrives.

Dwarf hamsters don't need to be inoculated or micro-chipped. The ethical care and responsible commitment required for these tiny little animals to be spared suffering, and to be given the proper care and happy life that they deserve is up to you. You; the human parent of a dwarf hamster that will depend entirely on you for food, water, hygienic care, love and attention for the duration of its life!

The mere fact that you are reading this book is an indication that you intend to be a proud and responsible human parent to a lucky dwarf hamster (or two, or maybe even a few), so here's to happy dwarf hamster days!

Chapter 1: About Dwarf Hamsters

Classification and Origin

Dwarf hamsters are classified as Phodopus, a genus of rodents in the hamster subfamily Cricetinae. They have become popular household pets with small animal lovers and are quite readily available because they breed easily in captivity.

Dwarf hamsters originate from Mongolia, Siberia, China and Kazakhstan inhabiting forests and semi-desert environments and can thrive in extreme conditions. Populations are widespread and abundant and they are not listed with any concern by any international conservation organisations. Their ecology and population dynamics are not well understood, but biologists currently recognise three species of dwarf hamsters, namely:

Sungorus, commonly known as:
- Djungarian (or Dzhungarian) Hamster
- Russian White or Russian Winter White Hamster
- Winter White Dwarf Hamster
- Siberian Hamster
- Striped Hairy-Footed Hamster
- Striped Desert Hamster

Campbelli, commonly known as:
- Djungarian (or Dzhungarian) Hamster
- Campbell's Dwarf Hamster
- Campbell's Desert Hamster

Roborovskii, commonly known as:
- Desert Hamster
- Roborovski Dwarf Hamster
- Roborovski's Desert Hamster
- Robo Dwarf Hamster

In the wild, dwarf hamsters remain underground during the day to avoid predators. They are active throughout the year and do not hibernate. Dwarf hamsters feed on seeds, fruits and vegetation but will also include insects in their diet. Like other hamsters, dwarf hamsters have a round body shape, short tails and elongated cheek pouches that allow them to carry food gathered back to their burrows.

Some publications as well as breeders include the Chinese Dwarf Hamster as part of the genus, but they are in fact of the genus Cricetidae, which includes hamsters, voles, lemmings, rats and mice. This genus has over six hundred species originating throughout the Americas, Asia and Europe.

Chinese dwarf hamsters physically resemble mice more than they do hamsters. Unscrupulous breeding has introduced hybrid variations of dwarf hamster where recognised species of dwarf hamster have been bred with Chinese dwarf hamsters.

Because Chinese dwarf hamsters are not actually of the same genus as dwarf hamsters and they differ in appearance, characteristics and temperament, information on keeping a Chinese dwarf hamster as a pet will not be included in this book.

General Facts of Each Species

Russian Winter White Dwarf Hamster
Genus Phodopus, species Sungorus, commonly referred to by any number of names as listed previously in the introduction will be referred to the Russian Winter White dwarf hamster for the rest of this book. The Russian Winter White dwarf hamster is often confused with the Campbell's dwarf hamster.

The Russian Winter White dwarf hamster originates from Russian and Asia. Typically ball shaped, they are about half the size of a Syrian hamster. Their average length is 7.5 to 10 centimetres or 3 to 4 inches and their average weight ranges from 19 to 45 grams or .067 to 1.59 ounces for males and 19 to 36 grams or .67 to 1.27 ounces for females. It is quite normal for their body weight to fluctuate considerably throughout the year and you can find it to be at the lowest during the winter months. In captive human care they tend to be slightly heavier on average than in the wild.

The Russian Winter Whites have a soft fur coat and furry paws. Generally, they come in five colours, namely normal (grey/brown) agouti, normal pearl, sapphire, sapphire-pearl and marbled. A wide range of additional colours are appearing on the market, but these different varieties are as a result of hybrid crossings. Their coats have a thick dark grey dorsal stripe that runs the full length of their bodies, from the crown of the head to the tail. In the wild their coats begin to thicken and to change colour as winter approaches, becoming lighter and lighter until it is almost pure white in colour. This change of colour in the wild between seasons has evolved to serve as a form of camouflage to escape predators. In the safety of captive human care, many Russian Winter Whites lose this colour changing process.

Irrespective of the natural colour of Russian Winter Whites (excluding hybrids), the mouth area up to the whiskers and the ears are a brighter colour than the rest of the coat. The throat, limbs, tail and underbelly are generally white, the ears have a pinkish tint and the outer edge of the ears and the eyes have a black lining.

In the wild the Russian Winter Whites dig tunnels of about 1 metre or 3.2 feet deep that lead to ground burrows where they store food, sleep, raise their young and hide from predators. They have elongated cheek pouches that extend to their shoulders that allow them to store food they gather and bring it back to their burrows. There may be multiple burrows and about six tunnel entrances that are kept open in the summer months. During the winter months the dwarf hamsters will leave only one entrance open, and close all of the others. During the heat of the summer months the burrows are lined with moss that provides a soft, cool interior. Animal fur and wool is scavenged to line the burrows during winter to provide a soft, warm interior.

Russian Winter Whites breed all year around in the wild and in captivity. The females' oestrous cycle lasts for four days, every four days. After mating and conception, the female will usually give birth to four to eight pups after twenty five days and can mate and conceive again on the same day that she gives birth. This process of rapid conception and a high birth rate has evolved to ensure the survival of the species considering that they have many predators in the wild. Pups are weaned and leave their mother before the next litter of pups is born.

Winter whites have an average lifespan of two years.

Campbell's Dwarf Hamster
Genus Phodopus, species Campbelli, also referred to as Campbell's desert hamster, will be referred to the Campbell's dwarf hamster for the rest of this book. The species name Campbelli and the common name Campbell's was given to this little dwarf hamster by Oldfield Thomas in honour of Charles William Campbell, who collected the first specimen in Mongolia in July, 1902.

The Campbell's dwarf hamster is often confused with the Russian Winter White dwarf hamster.

The Campbell's dwarf hamster originates from the steppes and semi-desert regions of Kazakhstan, Mongolia, China and Russia. They are closely related to the Russian Winter White dwarf hamster, but can be distinguished from the Russian Winter White by their ears, which are much smaller, their dorsal stripe that is narrower and their underbelly which is covered by grey fur.

Campbell's vary considerably in size in the world depending on their location, but their average length is about 10 centimetres or 4 inches and average weight ranges from 40 to 60 grams or 1.5 to 2 ounces for males and 30 to 50 grams or 1 to 1.7 ounces for females. In captive human care they tend to be slightly heavier on average than in the wild.

In the wild, Campbell's are coloured in either grey or brown with white fur around their lips, on their cheeks and on the top of their hind and fore paws. They have a narrow dark dorsal strip that runs from their tail to the nape of their neck. Their coat does not change colour in winter.

In the wild, Campbell's dig tunnels up to three feet long that lead to burrows that are lined with scavenged animal fur or wool and dry grass. They store food, sleep, raise their young and hide from predators in their burrows. These burrows have interconnecting tunnels and four to six entrance tunnels. Campbell's have elongated cheek pouches that extend to their rear legs that allow them to store food they gather and bring it back to their burrows.

There is a fixed breeding season that begins during April in the wild, but in captivity Campbell's will breed throughout the year. In the wild three to four litters are produces thought the breeding season, but in captivity a female can have up to eighteen litters in one year. The gestation period is eighteen to twenty days and the male will generally assist with the birthing process, pulling pups from the birth canal and cleaning them. In the days immediately following the birth of the pups the male will assist by bringing food for the mother and later the pups as well.

Campbell's have an average lifespan of 2 years.

Roborovski Dwarf Hamster

Genus Phodopus, species Roborovskii, commonly referred to by any of number of names as listed previously in the introduction will be referred to as the Roborovski dwarf hamster for the rest of this book. The species name Roborovskii and the common name Roborovski was given to this little dwarf hamster in honour of Russian exhibitioner, Lieutenant Vsevolod Roborovski, who first discovered them on an expedition in July 1894 and made notes of them in his journal.

The Roborovski dwarf hamsters originate from the desert regions of Kazakhstan, Mongolia and Russia and are the smallest of the three dwarf hamster species. The desert environments that they originate from are prone to extreme temperatures through all seasons. As a result of these harsh environments, Roborovski's have evolved spherical compact bodies that provide excellent insulation in the form of thick fur and body fat to protect them from extreme cold. During these periods of extreme cold they adopt a characteristic hunched posture with their head and paws tucked under their belly, while fluffing their fur to increase insulation.

During periods of extreme heat they flatten themselves on their underbelly and splay all four paws out away from their body. They also groom their fur into clumps, exposing areas of skin to allow air to flow through their coat. In addition they have evolved a sophisticated ability to conserve water in these arid environments by maintaining low evaporative body fluid rates and concentrated urine. Their average length is 4.5 to 5 centimetres or 1.8 to 2 inches and their average weight ranges from 20 to 25 grams or .71 to .88 ounces for males and 14 to 20 grams or 0.5 to 0.71 ounces for females. In captive human care they tend to be slightly heavier on average than in the wild.

Apart from their small size, other features that distinguish Roborovski's from the other two species of dwarf hamster are white 'eyebrow' spots above both eyes and the lack of any dorsal stripe. In the wild they are generally a grey-brown or sandy coloured. In the wild, Roborovski's dig tunnels up to 1.8 meters or 6 feet deep that lead to burrows where they store food, sleep, raise their young and hide from predators. Roborovski's have a fixed breeding season that begins during April and continues to September in the wild, but in captivity Roborovski's will breed throughout the year. In the wild three to four litters are produced through the breeding season. The gestation period is twenty to twenty two days.
Roborovski's have an average lifespan of three years.

Chapter 2: Deciding on a Dwarf Hamster as a Pet

Dwarf hamsters are small fragile little animals, but never the less sentient beings that can feel pain and suffering - even if it is inflicted unintentionally. It is vital that you thoroughly understand what to expect if you become the human parent of a dwarf hamster. Once you have acquired a dwarf hamster as a pet, you have a daily responsibility to that small little animal for up to four years because it will rely completely on how you care for it for its survival.

A dwarf hamster should never be given to a child as a pet to care for without permanent adult supervision because a child could easily forget to feed its dwarf hamster every day, provide clean water, not notice signs of illness or even injure the dwarf hamster unintentionally when playing with it. Apart from the pain, cruelty and potential threat of a horrible death to the dwarf hamster, the realisation that the dwarf hamster has been injured or died because of the actions (or inactions) of the child can be extremely traumatising to the child and can cause feelings extreme guilt. Children do not do not have the maturity to accept responsibility for the care for such a small fragile animal and to give a dwarf hamster to a child with the full responsibility of caring for it amounts to irresponsible parenting and potential animal cruelty. Parents are adults, and if your child wants a dwarf hamster and you are not willing to get involved in the daily care and supervision of the dwarf hamsters daily well being, refuse your child's request; say "No"- it's that simple!

Dwarf hamsters make good pets for adults and late-teens.

It is important to note that dwarf hamsters, like other fur-covered pets, can cause allergic reactions in humans. If you or a family member is prone to animal fur related allergies this must be taken into consideration before you decide to acquire a dwarf hamster as a pet.

Characteristics and Personality of each Species

Each of the three species of dwarf hamsters come with their own set of characteristics and personality which must be taken into consideration when deciding on which species best suits your lifestyle and expectations.

Russian Winter White Dwarf Hamster

Russian Winter White dwarf hamsters are found on the pet market in Europe and North America, but most are either hybrid or a Campbell's dwarf hamsters sold as Russian Whiter Whites. Pure bred Russian Winter Whites are generally only available from reputable breeders. In captivity they are available in their natural colours as well as a range of colours that are the result of captive breeding. They are easy to tame and are considered an excellent choice for novice dwarf hamster owners as they are easy to maintain and are not aggressive to people. They also are tolerant of living with other members of their species under certain conditions. If you have a breeding female among strange males she will definitely show aggression towards males during gestation and after the birth of her pups. If you have a breeding female it is best that she is separated from all other dwarf hamsters. Dwarf hamsters in captivity have no specific breeding season and breed very easily, you could buy a Winter White without knowing that she is in gestation as they do not look much different during this time. Breeding dwarf hamsters is covered in a later chapter.

Russian Winter Whites can be kept alone, in same sex pairs or in communities. If you want to keep them in pairs or communities it is best that you introduce them when they are only a few weeks old. Female pairs or communities are more successful because females are not territorial and do not have scent glands. Males are territorial and have scent glands for marking territory. Territorial fights can break out among males in any living enclosure, but if males are kept together in a small enclosure fighting over territory, food, living space (like exercise wheels, food bowls, bedding, etc) is almost inevitable. In some instances these fights can be to the death, so it is best to keep males over two months old separate.

In female pairs or communities there may be squabbles, but unless these squabbles are ongoing or severe causing injury there is no need for alarm. If the squabbles are ongoing or cause injury it is best to separate the dwarf hamsters. Consider if the living enclosure that you have provided is adequate to house a pair or community. You can try introducing them again after a few days, but if the squabbling starts again it is best to separate the dwarf hamsters permanently.

Like the other two species of dwarf hamsters, Russian Winter Whites do not hibernate. Because they originate from regions where the winter days are short, the nights long and the temperatures very cold, in the wild they spend less time outside of their burrows. In captivity they may still instinctively be inclined to spend less time out of their hamster houses.
They are nocturnal animals and will be more alert and inclined to feed and play from early evening to dawn. In captivity however this instinctive behaviour can change.

Russian Winter Whites, like all dwarf hamsters, move very quickly - so although they are easy to tame and handle, it is vital that when you are spending time playing with your dwarf hamster outside of its hamster enclosure you keep its agility and speed in mind. It is best to take your dwarf hamster into an enclosed area or closed room that offers no escape route. In addition, no other pets should have access to this area while your dwarf hamster is out of its enclosure. You don't want your dwarf hamster disappearing and being lost, or ending up as a meal for your cat or dog.

Apart from agility and speed, Russian Winter Whites are very curious little animals, so it is vital that you include a lot of action objects in your dwarf hamsters living enclosure like at least one exercise wheel, lots of tunnels, obstacles for your dwarf hamster to run under or climb over and instead of placing all the food in one place, spread and hide some around the enclosure to allow your dwarf hamster to search for its food. That food-finding challenge will make for one happy dwarf hamster!

Because of their relaxed and sociable nature, Russian Winter Whites are quite noisy, chattering and squawking and squeaking amongst themselves if in groups or pairs, and even on their own you will definitely hear your little dwarf hamster. You can say they have a big personality!

Campbell's Dwarf Hamster
The Campbell's dwarf hamster, like its' very close relative the Russian Winter White, are readily found on the pet market in Europe and North America. In captivity they are available in their natural colours as well as a range of colours that are the result of captive hybrid breeding. They are easy to tame and are considered an excellent choice for dwarf hamster owners who have some previous experience with dwarf hamsters as pets. They are easy to maintain and are generally not aggressive to people once they have become familiar with your scent and you and your dwarf hamster have come to an agreement on how you remove it from its living enclosure.

Campbell's are more territorial than other dwarf hamster species and can become defensive to humans as well as other dwarf hamsters when protecting their living enclosure. Aggression is almost always commonplace with females in gestation or with pups. Breeding females are best separated from other dwarf hamsters and you should also keep your distance from her, only replacing food and water in her living enclosure but avoiding any contact with her and her pups.

Same sex pairs or individuals can also become defensive to humans when protecting their territory. Initial signs of aggression are squeaking and swatting at you with their paws, and if you do not retreat they can actually bite you.

This is not necessarily a reason to overlook Campbell's as a pet because it is instinctive territorial behaviour or fear-based behaviour and it is up to you as the pet owner to learn how to handle them. Generally, once removed from their living enclosure, they are docile and easy to handle and play with. You can easily work around their instinctive territorial trait by the manner in which you approach your dwarf hamster when removing it from its living enclosure for play-time without invoking fear and territorial behaviour.

Firstly, ensure that the hamster house in the living enclosure is easily accessible and that the dwarf hamster will see any approach, and not be faced with suddenly being 'dug out' of a corner because that will definitely startle your dwarf hamster and result in it biting you.

If your dwarf hamster is out of its hamster-house when you approach it, observe its body language. If it starts scurrying around and squeaking at you or swats at you, retreat. Remember that dwarf hamsters get to recognise you by smell, so you don't want your dwarf hamster to associate your scent with stress and fear.

Instead, train your Campbell's to come out of corners or its hamster-house voluntarily by introducing a drinking mug, ladle or and other safe hollow receptacle into its living environment and once it has climbed in, slowly lift it out and away from the living enclosure before you handle it. In this way you are safely removing your dwarf hamster from its territory and allowing it to be aware of what is happening and so feel safe. Always use the same receptacle.

Most Campbell's will very quickly recognise the receptacle as an indication that play-time has arrived and happily hop in to be airlifted from their enclosure. This process will initially take a bit of patience, but the end result will be well worth the effort.

Although Campbell's are instinctively territorial, if pups have parents who are fiercely territorial, this trait will definitely be passed on.

Campbell's can be kept alone, in same sex pairs or in communities, as long as pairs or communities are introduced in the first few weeks of their life. Their territorial behaviour can cause them to reject other dwarf hamsters if they have matured. Both males and females have scent glands to mark their territory as well as to leave a scent trail as they move around. Campbell's have very poor eye sight and in the wild, this scent trail is used to easily find their way back to their burrow while out foraging. Their scent trail can last for up to eight days.

You may notice that if you take your Campbell's into an unfamiliar environment it will begin to frantically groom itself. This is to transfer scent form the scent glands located on its face, behind its ears and on its check pouches to its paws. This allows the dwarf hamster to always find its way back to the point it started moving around from by following the scent trail it left behind from its paws.

In existing communities there may be squabbles, but unless these squabbles are ongoing or severe causing injury there is no need for alarm. If the squabbles are ongoing, exhibit signs of obvious bullying or cause injury it is best to separate the dwarf hamsters permanently.

Like the other two species of dwarf hamsters, Campbell's do not hibernate. Because they originate from regions where the winter days are short, the nights long and the temperatures very cold, in the wild they spend less time outside of their burrows. In captivity they may still instinctively be inclined to spend less time out of their hamster-houses.

They are nocturnal animals and will be more alert and inclined to feed and play from early evening to dawn. In captivity however, this instinctive behaviour can change.

Campbell's, like all dwarf hamsters, move very quickly and are very agile, so once you have mastered lifting your dwarf hamster from its living enclosure and are able to handle it, it is vital that play time is restricted to an enclosed area or closed room that is free of any escape routes. Ensure that no other pets have access to this area while your dwarf hamster is out of its enclosure. Again, you don't want your dwarf hamster disappearing and being lost, or ending up as a meal for your cat or dog.

Apart from agility and speed, Campbell's - like Russian Winter Whites, are very curious little animals, so it is vital that you include a lot of action objects in your dwarf hamsters living enclosure like at least one exercise wheel, lots of tunnels, obstacles for your dwarf hamster to run under or climb over and instead of placing all the food in one place, spread and hide some around the enclosure to allow your dwarf hamster to search for its food. That food-finding challenge will make for one happy dwarf hamster!

Roborovski Dwarf Hamster
Roborovski dwarf hamsters are quite easily found on the pet market in Europe and North America. In captivity they are available in their natural colours as well as a range of colours that are the result of captive breeding. They are notably smaller than Russian Winter

White and Campbell's dwarf hamsters and have no dorsal stripe. Naturally timid and shy little animals, Roborvski's can be sensitive to loud noises, bright light and can become anxious. They are also extremely fast and their small size allows them to escape through the smallest of spaces if startled, so they are recommended as pets for people who prefer to observe them in their living enclosure rather than for people looking for a dwarf hamster to play with. Roborovski's do interact with humans, but prefer interaction like climbing up your arm and all over you at will rather than being picked up and handled. This type of explorative interaction will allow your dwarf hamster to become more tame and accustomed to your scent. Roborovski's are not inclined to form bonds of affection with their human parents like Russian Winter White and Campbell's can, but they will seldom bite and will rather bolt if scared than take a nip at you.

Roborovski's are more tolerant than Russian Winter White's and Campbell's of living with other members of their species, especially in family communities. In general they are not as aggressive and fighting does not often occur. If fighting does breakout though, they must be separated immediately to prevent injury or death. Despite being tolerant of other dwarf hamsters, Roborovski's do prefer a solitary life.

If you have a breeding female among a community or paired with a single male she may begin to show aggression towards the male or other dwarf hamsters a few days before birthing, and after the birth – becoming intolerant to any approach towards her nest and pups. It is advised that you also keep your distance from the female and her new pups, replacing food and water without disturbing her. If you have a breeding female it is best that she is separated from all other dwarf hamsters. Dwarf hamsters in captivity have no specific breeding season and breed very easily, you could buy a Roborovski female without knowing that she is in gestation as they do not look much different during this time. Breeding dwarf hamsters is covered in a later chapter.

Like the other two species of dwarf hamsters, Roborovski's do not hibernate and are nocturnal, becoming more alert and inclined to feed and play from early evening to dawn. In captivity however, this instinctive behaviour can change.

Roborovski's move exceptionally fast and are excellent climbers. They should not be exposed to children as they startle easily and do not like being handled. They are best observed rather than being handled, but if you want to coax them out of their living enclosure it is vital that you take your dwarf hamster into an enclosed area or closed room that offers no escape route. In addition, no other pets should have access to this area while your dwarf hamster is out of its enclosure. With their small size, exceptional speed and excellent climbing skills, your Roborovski could disappear in seconds resulting in it being permanently lost, injured or even killed. Because of their exceptional speed and climbing abilities it is vital that their living enclosure is spacious and includes a lot of action objects, at least one exercise wheel, lots of tunnels and obstacles for your dwarf hamster to run under or climb over. Roborovski's are known to spend hours on their exercise wheel and even fall asleep on their wheel. Also offer them foraging opportunities by hiding food all around their enclosure instead of placing all the food in one place.

With a living enclosure well-stocked with hiding places, action objects, many tunnels, hidden food and more you will find your Roborovski dwarf hamster will give you many hours of entertainment when you just sit back and observe the play and antics of this small little animal.

Hybrid Breeds

Hybrid dwarf hamsters are readily available on the pet market in Europe and North America. Hybrids are the result of breeding two similar species to achieve a specific result like variations in size or in coat colours, or to develop various character traits. This is usually done by breeders who base their choice of breeding dwarf hamsters with intention. Hybrids dwarf hamsters can also be the result of negligent owners who unintentionally breed between species by not separating males and females. In dwarf hamsters, only the Russian Winter Whites and Campbell's will cross breed.

Hybrid breeding is not to be confused with inbreeding. Inbreeding is breeding amongst direct family members - parents with off-spring, litter mates with each other and with off-spring from the same parents from previous litters. Inbreeding dwarf hamsters is covered in a later chapter.

Albino dwarf hamsters are not hybrid and can be found in all three species. Albino's have pure white fur all over their body that does not change colour, pink skin (visible on paws, ears and nose as well as under fur) and clear red eyes. Albinism is a gene passed down certain family lines to offspring.

Russian Winter Whites natural colouring is agouti and sapphire. There can be patterns of pearl and marble in both of the solid coat colours creating normal pearl, sapphire, sapphire-pearl and marbled.

Hybrid Russian Winter White colours include, mandarin, mushroom, orange/pudding, moscow and brown.

Campbell's are naturally coloured either grey or brown with white fur around their lips, on their cheeks and on the top of their hind and fore paws. There are, however, a further ten hybrid coat colours that are recognised. These are agouti (natural grey-brown with white underside), white-face (agouti with a white face), husky (pale salmon body with white face), pied (agouti with random white patches on the body and face), platinum (white-face at birth with body fur fading to white), head spot (pure white with a single colour spot on the head), dark-eared white (white with grey underbelly and ears), pure white and red-eyed (caramel coat with chocolate underbelly and dark brown eyes).

The pro's of buying hybrid dwarf hamsters is that their colours can be fascinating and will definitely draw attention from fans. The con's are that the characteristics and personality of hybrid dwarf hamsters is not always predictable. If you would prefer a specific temperament or social behaviour it is best to buy a hybrid from a reputable breeder who knows the family line rather than from a pet store that has no knowledge of the dwarf hamster's linage.

Because of the fascination with hybrid breeds colouring, hybrid breeding has become considered torture-breeding (which covers the illegal breeding of all animals, reptiles and birds) and is forbidden by law in several European countries, including Germany and Austria. There are many unscrupulous breeders who breed various pet types, including dwarf hamsters en-masse with very little consideration for the wellbeing of the breeding pairs, or their off-spring. They put profit before anything else and flood the pet trade with sickly or genetically compromised pets.

Making the Right Buying Choices

Now that you have more information on the characteristics and personality of each dwarf hamster species, including the pro's and con's of hybrid dwarf hamsters, you are in a position to decide on which species will best suit your household routines and your expectations. Where you choose to buy your new dwarf hamster from is also very important because it can have an impact on your experience as the human parent of a dwarf hamster.

Breeders
Buying a dwarf hamster from a reliable breeder where you can go and see the breeding environment and breeding pairs is always going to be your best choice. People who have developed a love for dwarf hamsters and practice ethical breeding standards will welcome you to view their breeding area and will be able to give you invaluable insight into the linage of your new purchase as well as information on how best to care for your dwarf hamster. They will almost always offer you tips and advice on dwarf hamsters that they have acquired over their time breeding and caring for dwarf hamsters.

Rescue Shelters
Although there are not many shelters that take in small pets like dwarf hamsters, they certainly do exist. An Internet search will give you information on any rescue shelters in your area that take in small pets like dwarf hamsters. If there is a shelter close to you, it is an excellent ethical choice to rescue an unwanted animal and give it another chance. It does, however, come with some risk as the shelter will have no details on where the dwarf hamster was bred, and sometimes no genuine information on why it was brought to the shelter.

This should not put an experienced dwarf hamster parent off though, or even a novice who has made an informed and committed decision to bring a dwarf hamster into their home. Any rescued pet often requires patience when they are first brought home because they can be quite traumatised by their previous experiences. Many pets in rescue shelters were impulse-buys or gifts that went stale and the animal ended up being dumped at a rescue shelter. All that is required is for you to give the little animal some time to adjust to their new environment, familiarise them with your scent when replacing water and food and not make any attempt to pick them up until they appear calmer and less anxious.

That done, you can then approach them in the manner best suited to the species. If they react with fear or aggression, back-off and give them a bit more time. You will find that with patience and care, you could end up with a wonderful little dwarf hamster that will reward you with hours of entertainment and even affection.

Pet Stores

Buying from a pet store is the general option for most people, especially first-time dwarf hamster human parents. Many pet stores do practice their trade along ethical lines and the owners have a great love of all type of pets and are very knowledgeable on a broad range of pets. There are many other pet store owners who buy their living 'stock' from shady breeders with little concern about the welfare of the pets they sell, and even little concern about the money taken from customers who end up with a very sickly pet that in many instances, dies shortly after purchase even with intervention from a veterinarian.

Another risk posed by buying form a pet store is that sales assistants often do not have much knowledge of dwarf hamsters and will incorrectly identify the species or sex. If you do not have the technical knowledge either, you could end up buying the opposite of what you wanted. In addition, you could also be sold a female in gestation because it is not always obvious from appearance that a dwarf hamster is carrying pups.

Pet stores also do not always have much information or tips to share with you about how to care for your new acquisition. If you have not researched how to set-up a dwarf hamster living enclosure, they could also advise you to buy items that are wholly unsuitable for a dwarf hamster - not only wasting your money, but items that could be harmful to the little animal. Dwarf hamster requirements cannot be compared to those of Syrian hamsters or other rodents simply because dwarf hamsters are so small and can be easily injured.

Classifieds or Online Adverts
Buying any pet, including dwarf hamsters, via online suppliers is really not a good choice. Many of these advertisers are the actual en-masse breeders who have no ethics and practice commercial breeding keeping animals in crowded unhygienic environments, or their agents. These animals are often fairly 'wild' when you get them because there is almost no human contact in commercial breeding - just cruelty and focus on moving the pups as quickly as possible for maximum profit.

You will have no idea of what type of dwarf hamster you are going to get, what its linage is, how healthy it is and what sex it is unless you have the technical knowledge. In that case you will be faced with having to refuse the little animal and that can lead to confrontation. Most classified and online sellers will agree to meet you at some public place for the exchange of cash for the little animal. Once you have paid, they drive off and that is the last that you will see of them!

Often people selling this way will send you pictures of the animal that you are going to buy and they ask for a down-payment. Many buyers of all kinds of pets transacted in this manner have been left shocked when they see that the picture and what they have paid for are not the same. Many of the animals very sick almost immediately or suffer from disabilities or behavioural problems.

Deciding on Single or Multiples, Male or Female
Once you have decided on the species you want and where to buy your dwarf hamster from, you need to decide if you are going to buy a single dwarf hamster, a pair or a community.

If you opt for a pair or want to create a family, it is vital to bear in mind that dwarf hamsters tend to accept each other more readily if they are introduced in the early weeks of their life. Also consider the species because not all species are tolerant of cohabitation. If you are a novice dwarf hamster parent, or you are buying a hybrid, it is best to buy a single dwarf hamster to avoid any unpleasant experiences.

Most species pair best when you put two young females together. Males do not always tolerate each other well even if introduced in the early weeks of their life, especially if the living enclosure does not offer adequate space for each of them to have their own territory, living space, food and water, exercise wheel, tunnels, etc. In other words, if you want to house two males together you must ensure that their living enclosure has enough space to accommodate them each with their own hamster-house and all the other things they need to be happy, without them getting in each other's way. Food and water must also be spaced well apart so that each little fellow can feed and drink in his own territory.

An important point to keep in mind if you intend on buying in multiples, is that dwarf hamsters are not very easy to sex, especially to the untrained eye. If you are buying from a pet store, rescuing from a shelter or buying online you could end up with two males instead of two females or any other permutation of sexes and if you yourself are inexperienced you could find yourself facing compatibility problems within a few days of bringing your new dwarf hamsters home.

Checking for Sickness or Physical Defects
Whether you are buying a single dwarf hamster or multiples, ensuring good health and physical well being of each little animal is vital. Bringing an unhealthy pet into your home can be costly as well as heartbreaking. After so much planning and anticipation, to bring home a sickly pet is not what you want. Apart from costly

veterinarian bills, most small pets that are bought unhealthily generally die within the first few weeks of purchase by which time you have probably bonded to the little animal. No ethical pet trader would put a sickly animal on the market, so if you have bought a sickly or physically unsound dwarf-hamster you have probably been dealing with an unethical and unscrupulous trader.

This is one of the main reasons that buying dwarf hamsters (or any pets) from classified or online advertisers is not advised in the strongest of terms. Most of the animals they sell are from en-masse breeders who have no ethical breeding standards and practice commercial breeding for profit only. In the crowded, unhygienic conditions these animals are bred in, sickness is rife and left untreated and inbreeding common so physical and behavioural defects go unchecked. In most cases you will only see the animal on hand-over and you will not have enough time to properly look it over before the seller disappears.

If you are buying from a breeder, pet store or rescue shelter there are a number of things to look out for and consider before you make your choice and purchase. Immediately walk away if the area where the dwarf hamsters are kept is dirty and smells very bad. There will always be a different smell in any area where lots of animals are kept, and that may be unfamiliar to a novice pet owner, but if the smell is pungent it is most certainly a sign of poor care and hygiene in the enclosures. Enclosures that are not cleaned out regularly will smell of a combination of urine, faeces and rotting food - and that is what you must avoid because there will almost certainly be sickly animals housed in conditions like this where bacteria is rife and parasites proliferate. Pet traders of this kind should in all honesty be reported to authorities governing the trade of animals in your area because keeping pets trapped in unhygienic conditions is animal cruelty. Traders like this should not be supported; they should be closed down without question!

When looking at the dwarf hamsters for sale, don't hesitate to ask questions and carefully listen to the answers that you get from the seller. If you are buying from a breeder and they select a few dwarf hamsters for you to choose from away from the breeding enclosures, ask if you can see the breeding enclosures. If they deny you access, ask them directly why not. They could be bringing you the healthier looking dwarf hamsters while keeping you away from unhealthy ones and many diseases are contagious. Your dwarf hamster could be healthy now, but incubating bacteria in its body that will cause sickness and even death within a few days. If you already have other dwarf hamsters at home, you could unintentionally be exposing them transmittable sicknesses. Some sicknesses and parasites are transmittable to other domestic pets as well as humans.

Once you're satisfied with the living conditions your new addition comes from you want to identify that each dwarf hamster you choose is healthy. Dwarf hamsters are stocky or thick-set with a rounded type body shape, short tails and visible check pouches. If they have been awoken for you to view them, they should still be bright-eyed and active within minutes. Lethargy is generally a sign of sickness. If the seller tells you that the dwarf hamster is lethargic because it has just been awoken, proceed with caution! Remember that in the wild dwarf hamsters, like all rodent species, have many predators so they can become alert and escape within split seconds; they are not a species that is inclined to laze about.

Healthy dwarf hamsters will have a full and healthy coat of fur, free from matting or patching, they will walk or run without effort and their breathing will look normal (almost unnoticeable).

Blatant symptoms of sickness in dwarf hamsters to be aware of are nasal or eye discharge as well as obvious breathing difficulties (respiratory tract infections), obvious wetness under the tail (diarrhoea), patchy coat (skin mites), skin lesions and being underweight.

If the dwarf hamsters that you are viewing to make your choice appear healthy but fearful and a bit 'wild', remember that these little animals can be naturally skittish and can easily become anxious. Instinct carried over from their wild ancestry is to escape danger, and if they feel trapped, fear and anxiety can set in. Don't let that put you off – but do remember that you will have to give your new dwarf hamster or hamsters a good few days to settle into their new home before you can handle them. Some dwarf hamsters (like many baby pets) may not have had much exposure to humans because ethical breeders will not want to disturb the mothers and her pups.

Sicknesses in dwarf hamsters will be covered in more detail later in this book.

Chapter 3: Cost of Keeping a Dwarf Hamster

Although dwarf hamsters are very small animals, you must be willing to commit to the cost of providing a spacious and healthy living environment with accessories for feeding, drinking, stimulation, sleeping, hiding and exercise.

You have to clean their living environment weekly, replacing substrate (flooring cover), nesting material (bedding), chews (for gnawing to maintain healthy teeth), sand (for bathing) and daily food. You must also budget for veterinary care because it is not advised that you treat your dwarf hamster for any medical condition, be it cuts and scrapes or disease because they cannot be treated with medication (even topical) that can be used to treat cats, dogs or humans. Their small body weight can make these medications toxic and cause poisoning and death.

The biggest investment in your dwarf hamster is setting up a healthy living environment which can cost you anywhere from $18 to $100 or £13 to £75 for a cage or aquarium and $140 or £105 for quality accessories. Once you have made this layout though you should not have to spend anymore.

You can also save substantially if you opt to make your own accessories from cardboard, toilet roll holders, wood and coconut shells. This option is the better option if you are willing to put in the time because it is safer for your dwarf hamster.

Cost of a Dwarf Hamster

The cost of a dwarf hamster ranges from $2 to $20 or £1.50 to £15 depending on where you buy it from. Pet stores that obtain stock from commercial breeders are often over-stocked and you can buy a dwarf hamster for next-to-nothing. Breeders on the other hand will be more expensive, but they will be able to give you information of the dwarf hamster's linage as well as information on how to take care of it. Exotic hybrids bred specifically for colour combinations are expensive. Unfortunately their size, lifespan, characteristics and personality will not be predictable because they are the result of breeding between species. The hybrid dwarf hamster could still become a lovable, healthy and entertaining little pet though!

Initial Costs to Equip Living Environment

You must be willing to provide your newly acquired dwarf hamster with the biggest cage or aquarium that you can afford. Keeping it in a small environment with few accessories is cruel because it will lead to stress and can manifest in behavioural and health problems like pulling out its coat, gnawing at cage bars and fighting to the death if you have a pair or more.

A space of 75cm x 40cm x 40 cm or 29.5 inches x 15.75 inches x 15.75 inches for one dwarf hamster only is the minimum advised by experts on dwarf hamster care. The size can be bigger, but you must not go smaller. If you cannot afford a cage or aquarium of this size pass on acquiring a dwarf hamster as a pet.

Fancy plastic living environments produced specifically for dwarf hamsters and fitted with all types of fancy accessories in fancy colours are the most expensive option. They are, however, totally unsuitable to house your dwarf hamster! Generally they are too small, the accessories are fixed and so difficult to clean and sanitise, plastic contains deadly toxins that will be ingested by your dwarf hamster when it gnaws at the accessories, they retain heat and humidity making them a perfect environment for breeding bacteria and plastic is an environment nightmare. Don't buy plastic!

A glass aquarium or metal cage is the best option for dwarf hamsters. If you buy a metal cage, ensure that the bars are very closely spaced to prevent your dwarf hamster from squeezing through and escaping. Metal cages made for Syrian hamsters are not suitable for dwarf hamsters. Also ensure that the cage has a solid floor and not a wire or mesh floor because dwarf hamsters will injure their tine paws and toes on wire or mesh. If you opt for a glass aquarium, ensure that it has a well fitting cover that provides very good ventilation. A glass aquarium is the best option for a dwarf hamster because it is safe for tiny bodies and gives you a 360° view of your dwarf hamster's daily routines, play and antics.

Currently both metal cages and aquariums can cost you anywhere from $18 to $100 or £13 to £75 depending on quality and size. Remember to avoid any sharp or rough interior folds or protrusions because that will injure your dwarf hamster.

Accessories like a hamster-house can cost you virtually nothing if you make your own from cardboard or a cleaned and dried coconut shell (which provides an environment closer to nature), ladders made from wooden popsicles sticks and tunnels made from toilet roll holders. Many dwarf hamster owners also don't put food in a food bowl, but rather spread and hide food all about the living environment so that their dwarf hamster has to forage and search for food, once again emulating a lifestyle closer to its natural environment.

If you are not into DIY and want to buy accessories, always opt for stainless steel or ceramic. Avoid plastic accessories and anything painted because paints also contain toxins that can be ingested if gnawed at. Be willing to buy the best, most natural products that you can afford for your dwarf hamster. The estimated prices listed are based on wooden, ceramic, glass and stainless steel products, which are the most suitable.

A wooden exercise wheel that is the most safe for your dwarf hamster will cost in the region of $20 or £15, a ceramic sand bath (covered to prevent spillage) $30 or £22, ceramic food bowl (solid non-tip) $30 or £22, glass water bottle with stainless steel tip $20 or £15, wooden hamster-house $15 or £11 and a wooden tunnel, bridge and hideout combination $25 or £19. That will give you an average cost for quality bought accessories of $140 or £105.

Daily Upkeep and Feeding

Your dwarf hamster will need to have the substrate floor covering as well as the nesting material provided for it to make a nest for sleeping and storing food in its hamster-house. There are many commercial brands of substrate and nesting material available from pet stores and retailers. Many of these products are unsuitable for dwarf hamsters so you must check the packaging carefully to see that it specifies that it is suitable for dwarf hamsters. These products can cost you anywhere from $6 to $20 or £4 to £15 depending on the size and quality you choose.

Again, you can save yourself money and guarantee your dwarf hamster's safety by making your own nesting material from shredded un-dyed, un-bleached and unscented toilet paper. Twelve single-ply toilet rolls will last you for months. You can also drop whole single sheets into your dwarf hamster's enclosure to allow it to do some of its own shredding! You can also make your own cheap and healthy substrate from un-dyed, un-bleached and unscented paper towels. A single roll of industrial sized paper towel sold at bulk suppliers of sanitary and hygiene equipment will also last for months.

Wooden chews that are necessary for your dwarf hamster to gnaw on to keep its teeth healthy are available from pet store and retailers for around $3 to $10 or £2 to £7.50. Sand for your dwarf hamster's sand bath will cost you about $10 or £7.50, but it will last you for quite a few months. It is important that you buy sand for dwarf hamsters specifically because sand with dust can cause respiratory problems, garden sand could contain toxins and sand for children's play is unsuitable.

Dwarf hamsters must be fed a diverse and healthy diet. There are quality mixes of grain and other essentials like nuts, dried fruit and mealworm available at pet stores and retailers. Always choose the best quality that you can afford. Considering that a dwarf hamster requires only a tablespoon of food a day, it will last for quite a while. Current prices range from $5 to $15 or £3.75 to £11.

Veterinary Costs

Veterinary costs can be difficult to predict because unlike cats and dogs, dwarf hamsters do not need to be vaccinated or micro-chipped. You could acquire a very healthy dwarf hamster that has almost no health issues over the course of its short life (an average two years), or you could acquire a dwarf hamster that has constant health issues.

In addition, not all veterinarians treat dwarf hamsters so you may have to travel some distance to find specialist veterinary care. Consultation fees vary from one veterinary practice to another, so you can budget an estimated $25 to $65 or £20 to £50 for a consultation, treatment and medication.

Medication for dwarf hamsters will be prescribed in very small doses so the cost would not be high. Because of the low body mass of dwarf hamsters, surgery is very rare because of the potential complication with anaesthetic.

Chapter 4: Creating a Healthy Living Environment

In the wild, dwarf hamsters live in territories that they claim above ground, and also in burrows that they dig underground that are accessed by deep tunnels that they dig from the ground surface. There are a number of underground burrows that are connected by underground tunnels. The surface area of the territory, tunnels and burrows is quite substantial, giving each dwarf hamster a fairly large area of living space to run around in. Although your dwarf hamster's wild ancestors may be a good many years since, it is vital that you provide your dwarf hamster with as big a living environment as you can afford. Just because they are small in size does not mean that they need only a small area to live in!

If you intend to keep more than one dwarf hamster you must increase the living environment accordingly because overcrowding is a very big stress trigger for dwarf hamsters and an environment that does not allow for each to have its own space will definitely lead to fights, often to the death.

Many commercially manufactured enclosures and accessories for rodents are not suitable for dwarf hamsters because of the small size of dwarf hamsters. Even products manufactured for Syrian hamsters are not always suitable. Another factor to bear in mind is that commercially manufactured pet products are often imported from countries where there is very little to no legislation around the chemical components of paints, plastics and similar components. Most of these products are produced with focus on the aesthetics, creating brightly coloured items and items that look cute and appeasing to the eye. They are not produced with any scientific input and therefore little concern for the pet that will be exposed to the product, or for the consumer who will buy the product.

A dwarf hamster is not a fashion item! It is a living sentient being that can feel discomfort, pain and suffering. In the wild their living environment is obviously created by and from nature; in every way try to create as natural an environment as possible for your new furry little friend or friends. Avoiding plastic and painted items is a good place to start, and you will discover that the aesthetically appealing items (only to humans that is) are actually more costly than more natural options.

Many imported plastic products available on the market contain toxins, as do many paints. Although your local legislators may have banned the use of these toxins in products, many countries exercise very little, if any control over the use of toxins in manufacture. Dwarf hamsters (and all other rodents) are naturally inclined to gnaw away at most things around them, and if their environment is filled with fancy items produced with toxins you could be writing out a death sentence unintentionally for your little dwarf hamster.

In addition, even ethically produced plastic does not breathe as natural products do so bacteria can become trapped in corners and ridges, creating a threat not only to your dwarf hamster, but to you and your other pets as well. Plastic has become an environmental nightmare worldwide, and if you care about your pet, yourself and the environment - plastic should be avoided as much as possible.

Selecting the Right Cage or Tank

Your cage, or tank, as well as all essential equipment, bedding and substrate and food should all be purchased and assembled before you bring your new dwarf hamster home.

Dwarf hamsters must be kept is a secure cage or tank that not only keeps them in, but also keeps them safe and sound from other pets or neighbouring predacious visitors. Never underestimate the ability of a dwarf hamster to slip through small gaps or openings, and never underestimate the determination of a cat (and the odd dog) to get into a dwarf hamster a cage!

Whether you opt for a cage or a tank, always choose the biggest that you can afford. A space of 75cm x 40cm x 40 cm or 29.5 inches x 15.75 inches x 15.75 inches for one dwarf hamster only is the minimum advised by experts on dwarf hamster care.

If you opt for a cage, make sure that the care is suitable for a dwarf hamster specifically and is not a general hamster cage. Because they are so small, dwarf hamsters can slip through the bars of most cages with ease. Also, select a cage with a solid floor and not a wire floor. Wire floors can injure the tiny feet of dwarf hamsters very badly. The area around a cage with bars can become very messy, as dwarf hamsters like to dig and love to have a sand bath if you provide one. You could end up with more cleaning than you anticipated!

Glass tanks specifically manufactured to house hamsters (and other rodents) are available, or you can buy a glass aquarium, which is equally suitable. A glass tank will protect your dwarf hamsters from drafts and from cold, keeps them from slipping through bars and also allows you a wonderful view to observe their activities, play and antics. A tank must be fitted with a secure mesh cover over the top that allows for excellent ventilation, but is strong enough to keep predatory intruders at bay and has no gaps that could allow your dwarf hamster an escape route.

There are fully equipped plastic hamster-homes available that come fitted with fixed plastic tubes, exercise wheels, feeding bowls and water bottles, but these are very expensive, are bacteria-traps and generally are too small for dwarf hamsters. Apart from the fact that they are not environmentally friendly, they are a totally unnatural environment for any animal because they are inclined to trap heat and humidity creating a bacteria-paradise! They are a health hazard to your dwarf hamster, yourself and your other pets unless you are willing to not only clean them out more than once a week, but also sterilise them as well with a bleach dilution at the same time. Cleaning and sterilising these hamster-homes is very difficult to do because most of the content is fixed and that makes it very difficult to access all ridges, corners and tubes properly. Don't buy them!

Finally, positioning your dwarf hamster's cage or tank is equally important. Make sure that the spot you choose is free from constant drafts, direct sunlight or sudden temperature changes. Also keep the cage out of view from other pets, particularly cats and dogs. Remember that dwarf hamsters are nocturnal, so they must be housed in a room that gets dark at night to accommodate their instinctive behaviour. Placing their cage in your living room where there is a television and lights on at night might suit you so that you can effortlessly watch their behaviour and play, but it will be most unsuitable for your dwarf hamster. Many dwarf hamsters are negatively affected by bright or flashing lights and loud sounds – so that idea won't work. Bear in mind that their nocturnal behaviour includes squeaking, scurrying, gnawing, digging and running on their exercise wheel (sometimes for hours). Unless you're a dead-sleeper, placing your dwarf hamster's cage or tank in your bedroom can result in a sleepless night for you!

Equipping the Living Environment

Once you have selected the cages or tank that best suits you must create a healthy living environment inside to keep your dwarf hamster healthy and happy. There are certain items that are essential and others that are nice add-on's, but always ensure that all interior equipment is safe for dwarf hamsters and will not cause injury to the tiny animal.

Essential equipment to create the right living environment for your dwarf hamster includes:

A hamster-house

- also referred to as a nesting box, provides your dwarf hamster with a good hiding place, a larder to store food collected in its cheek pouches, as well as a place where it can sleep feeling safe and sound. The house must be a hollow structure with a single small opening for entry that will create a safe and cosy space for your dwarf hamster. If you have a pair it's best to have two separate houses set apart in the living environment to avoid territorial fighting. Even if you have a single dwarf hamster, more than one hamster-house is preferable to give your dwarf-hamster variety. Remember that in the wild dwarf hamsters live in numerous underground burrows connected by tunnels.

There are many commercially produced hamster-houses on the market, with the majority being made of plastic. As mentioned previously, plastic is not a good choice because it is not only expensive and potentially toxic, but it is also difficult to clean and a can create a perfect environment for bacteria to proliferate. Painted houses should also be avoided because dwarf will gnaw at items in their living environment, and you don't want your dwarf hamster ingesting paint. There are pet accessory manufacturers who produce environmentally friendly wooden houses that are an excellent choice. A quick Internet search will give you details of suppliers in your area and many of them sell online.

In reality, you don't have to spend much money to provide your new dwarf hamster with an excellent hamster-house that will not cost you much at all other than a little of your time. You can make your own hamster-house using a small cardboard box and a toilet roll holder. These natural products are much more suitable, cost effective and are just as good as any commercially manufactured items.

To make a cardboard hamster-house it is best to use a plain small cardboard box free of outer printing (unless you can establish that the ink used for printing is non-toxic). Plain small cardboard boxes are readily available from craft and most hardware stores. You will also need to buy non-toxic glue, also available from craft and hardware stores. Cut a round circle out on one side of the box keeping it close to a corner edge using a craft knife. The circle must be cut to fit the circumference of a toilet roll holder. Completely seal all the box flaps to seal it. Fit the toilet roll holder into the hole, creating a downward slant, and there you have a perfect hamster-house with a cute entrance tunnel. You can also use two cardboard boxes made in the same way, but with a second circle cut into sides that face each other if they stand side-by-side. You can then join the two boxes with another toilet roll holder giving your dwarf hamster two houses. This is similar to the underground burrows they live in, in the wild that are connected by tunnels. Don't paint the box or tunnel, not even with water paints. Leave it natural and cover it with substrate to make it more interesting for your dwarf hamster, as it can dig about around its house as well. Your hamster-house will not last as long as a bought one, but it is so easy to make that you can construct a new one in a matter of minutes. The Internet has many 'how-to' videos to show you step-by-step.

Another natural and more durable hamster-house that is ideal to make is to use an empty coconut shell. Your dwarf hamster will love it and it will last longer than the cardboard option. All you need is a reasonable sized coconut that can either be split in half using a hammer and striking it on the centre line, or if you have a suitable power tool you can drill a hole through anywhere on the outer shell. If you are going to drill a hole, it must be big enough firstly to allow you to scoop out the coconut meat, and secondly to allow your dwarf hamster easy access. If you are going to halve the coconut, you must scrape out an arch in the shell on one side to give your dwarf hamster access to its house. Whichever method you choose, you must ensure that you scoop out all the coconut meat and then rinse the inside shell very well. The empty shell must then be dried by putting it out is the sun for a few days, or placing it in an oven at 150° Celsius or 300° Fahrenheit for an hour or two until it is completely dry. Although it requires more work than the cardboard option, a coconut shell is much more durable and will last much longer. It makes an excellent natural habitat for your dwarf hamster. The Internet also has many 'how-to' videos to show you step-by step.

Nesting Material
- must be made of soft and cosy materials that can be used to make a nest in the hamster-house or nesting box. There are many types of commercially manufactured nesting material available, but not all are suitable for dwarf hamsters. Never use cotton shreds, cotton-wool or hamster wool nesting as dwarf hamsters cannot digest cotton fibres, and if ingested it could kill your dwarf hamster by choking or by causing a digestive tract blockage. Also avoid any acrylic and synthetic materials and bits of wool. Apart from being indigestible choking hazards that can cause intestinal blockages, dwarf hamsters can easily become entangled in loose fibres and this can cause injury or death.

In addition, acrylic and synthetic shreds or wool has no breathing properties, so put inside your dwarf hamster's house or nesting box it will trap moisture and become a breeding ground for bacteria - creating a health hazard for you and your dwarf hamster.

The most suitable nesting material is plain unbleached, un-dyed, un-perfumed toilet paper. Usually sold in single-ply, it is soft, safe and cheap to buy. Simply tear it up into small bits, and then put in a few whole single sheets for your dwarf hamster to happily shred as well.

Water Bottle
- a water bottle is recommended to ensure that your dwarf hamster has constant access to clean water. A water bowl can easily be tipped over or become contaminated by soiled substrate when your dwarf hamster is digging. If a water bowl is tipped and your dwarf hamster is wet in the process, it can lead to sickness.

Water bottles can be fitted to metal cages by attaching them to the bars with spout on the inside and the bottle on the outside, making it easy to refill the bottle without disturbing the dwarf hamster. In glass aquariums, the bottles can be attached to the inside by suction cups, or suspended from the top cover. If you choose to suspend the water bottle, ensure that is placed low enough for your dwarf hamster to access it easily without having to stretch.

Most water bottles are made of plastic, some with a plastic spout and others with a metal spout. Always opt for a metal spout because of a dwarf hamsters' tendency to gnaw at everything. You definitely don't want your dwarf hamster ingesting potentially toxic pieces of plastic.

A far more ethical choice is to buy a glass water bottle with a metal spout. There are manufacturers who produce pet accessories that are made of recycled glass. Glass water bottles can be fitted to cages and aquariums in the same manner as plastic bottles are.

Food Dish
- the type and placement of your dwarf hamster's food dish is very important. Dwarf hamsters are very busy little animals, and a food dish placed on the floor could end up being tipped over or being filled with substrate as it scurries about the living environment.

Dishes are generally manufactured in plastic, stainless steel and ceramic. Choose a food dish that is sturdy, heavy and cannot be tipped over as your dwarf hamster may choose to sit in the food dish while feeding and accidently tip it over when it jumps out.

It is advisable to elevate the food dish by putting it on a stand to avoid the food becoming contaminated by substrate (which could be soiled).
As dwarf hamsters gnaw at everything, the food dish will be no exception. Avoid plastic food dishes as they are easily gnawed down and can contain toxins that will be ingested and can be toxic. Ceramic and stainless steel food dishes are gnaw-proof.

Exercise Wheel
- an exercise wheel is a vital accessory for your dwarf hamster's living environment to ensure that it stays healthy. Although dwarf hamsters are tiny animals, they are very active and can run up to 9 Kilometres or 5.5 miles in one night. They would never be able to run this distance freely in their living environment without an exercise wheel.

The minimum size exercise wheel recommended for a dwarf hamster is 6.5 inches or 16.5 centimetres, but 7.9 inches or 20 centimetres is recommended. It is vital that your dwarf hamster does not have an exercise wheel that is too small for them because that can cause back problems. Running on a small wheel will cause your dwarf hamster to run with an arched back, which over time will cause health problems. Running on a bigger wheel allows your dwarf hamster to run with its body flat, similar to running on the ground in the wild.

Dwarf hamster exercise wheels come in metal, plastic and the more ethical and natural option of wood. A metal exercise wheel is probably the most durable, and will not be gnawed at like plastic and wood. If you opt for metal, ensure that it is not painted. Plastic is never a good option because of the potential toxicity and effects on your dwarf hamster when it is gnawed at, as well as the negative impact discarded plastic has on the environment. Although a wooden exercise wheel will be gnawed at and may not have the endurance of a metal wheel, it is most certainly the best and most natural option! Remember, your dwarf hamster still has distant family living in the wild.

Dwarf hamsters must never be given an exercise wheel with rungs (most metal wheels have rungs). The inside of the exercise wheel for dwarf hamsters must be solid. Dwarf hamsters legs and paws are too small and fragile for a wheel with rungs (spaces between each diagonal bar on the inside of the wheel). Your dwarf hamster could easily injure or even break a limb on a wheel with rungs. In a small animal like dwarf hamsters, the trauma of a broken limb could lead to death.

Plastic and wooden wheels manufactured with a solid inside are quite readily available from pet stores as well as online pet equipment retailers. Some wheels come with a safety stand and closed rear wall to protect your dwarf hamster from falling from the wheel and becoming trapped, potentially causing injury. Wooden wheels with a cork interior are highly recommended because they allow your little dwarf hamster to get a solid grip, and the buoyancy of the cork surface is very kind to small limbs and paws as well as the tiny spine. The additional expense is well spent to ensure the safety and health of your dwarf hamster.

Depending on where you have placed your dwarf hamster's living environment, you must consider that some exercise wheels can be noisy, and with the dwarf hamster running for quite a few hours every night, it could be a source of sleepless nights for you. If your dwarf hamster is positioned close to where people are sleeping, it is well worth spending a bit extra to buy an exercise wheel that runs silently. If the wheel does become a bit noisy over time, a few drops of vegetable oil on the spindle should solve the problem. If the wheel starts rattling, check the attachments and if necessary, re-attach the wheel because it can become loose with all the use.

Substrate
- often also referred to as bedding, is spread over the floor of the living environment and is a substitute for the grassy environment that dwarf hamsters live in, in the wild. In a cage or tank the substrate serves as a source of stimulation for your dwarf hamster to run through and dig around in. It also absorbs urine and odour.

Substrate should be a minimum of 4 centimetres or 1.5 inches to 15 centimetres or 6 inches deep and must be loosely placed. If it is compacted it will not serve the purpose that it is intended for. The substrate must be comfortable for your dwarf hamster to live in. There are many types of commercially manufactured substrate available, and you can easily make your own.

Ensure that whatever your choice of substrate is, it is absorbent, free of any dyes, non-toxic and unscented. Scented and colourfully dyed products may be pleasant for humans but they are not at suitable for any animals, including dwarf hamsters.

Wood shavings are widely sold as substrate, but should be avoided (especially cedar and pine), as it is not very absorbent and can cause allergies and respiratory problems in both dwarf hamsters and humans. Likewise, sawdust and cat-litter must be avoided. Hay and dried chunks of corn-cobs are recommended by some experts, but neither are easily available.

There are many commercial brands of substrate available for dwarf hamsters from retailers and pet stores. It is best to do some research on the Internet of the brand quality as well as content available in your area before you make your choice.

You can make your own substrate using unprinted, un-dyed white paper that is shredded or torn into small pieces and then soaked in water to form a pulp. Once the paper has sufficiently broken down, all residual water must be squeezed out and the paper can then either be spread in a solid sheet and left out to dry, or shaped into fist-full balls and dried out. Once dry, the paper must again be broken into small pieces and can then be used as substrate. The type of paper that you use will dictate how successful your homemade substrate is. Hard papers, like those used for notebooks and office printing will not be very absorbent. The best paper to use is the bulk rolls of handtowels often used in public toilets to dry hands after washing. The paper on these rolls is quite rough and hard to the touch, not pure white because it is unbleached and highly absorbent. Although not available at general retailers, you will easily be able to buy these rolls of paper from bulk suppliers of sanitary and hygiene equipment.

Sandbox
 - a sandbox should be regarded as an essential and not an extra for your dwarf hamsters living environment. Dwarf hamsters keep themselves clean by rolling around in sand and then grooming themselves to remove excess body oils and anything that has become stuck to their coat. It is a source of stimulation, exercise and instinctive grooming for your dwarf hamster. Having a regular sand bath makes for a very happy little dwarf hamster! It is best that you buy a sand box with a cover, rather than an open bath because your dwarf hamster will be kicking the sand around and that can a make quite a mess.

There are ceramic sandboxes available and these are the best option because they are heavy enough to withstand your dwarf hamster's energetic hygiene routine. Plastic sandboxes are not only too light, but also can be gnawed at, exposing your dwarf hamster to ingesting potentially toxic material.

It is best to buy good quality sand, specially purposed for your dwarf hamsters bathing routine. It is vital that you avoid products packaged as 'dust' because this will cause respiratory problems for your dwarf hamster. Also avoid dust/sand combinations for the same reasons. Definitely do not use garden sand or sand sold for children's play. Garden sand can contain any number of toxins from herbicides and pesticides, as well as a host of other unwanted matter that can cause harm to your dwarf hamster. Even if you practice organic gardening, your neighbours don't and these toxins are carried from one property to another by the flow of rainwater. Children's play-sand often contains silica and is quite coarse; it is not suitable for dwarf hamsters.

Your dwarf hamster needs to take a sand bath on average three times a week. Whether you leave the sandbox permanently in the living environment or take it out after your dwarf hamster has had a bath, and put it back in two days later, is your choice. If it is left permanently in the enclosure, some dwarf hamsters will use it as a toilet, especially if it is placed quite a distance away from their hamster-house. Whether you see that as a pro or a con is again your choice. If your dwarf hamster does use the sandbox as a toilet you will obviously have to change the sand very regularly. If you choose to remove the sandbox, you can remove sand that looks soiled and then just top-up before putting it in the enclosure again.

Your dwarf hamster must never be bathed with water, as this will strip its coat of vital oils that serve to insulate the coat and keep your dwarf hamster warm. If you do bath your dwarf hamster with water it will almost certainly become sick and can even die. Only ever let a veterinarian wash your dwarf hamster if necessary, and if your dwarf hamster has been injured keep the wound clean and dry as instructed by a veterinarian.

If you find a dirty or soiled spot your dwarf hamster's coat that does not come clean after a sand bath, you can gently brush the coat with a dry toothbrush to remove the offending blemish.

Chews

- dwarf hamsters (like all rodents) have teeth that grow continuously and that is why you must provide them with items that they can chew on to prevent them from gnawing at the bars of their cage or at any other items in their living environment. The more healthy chews you provide, the less likely your dwarf hamster is to gnaw at things you don't want gnawed at. If a dwarf hamster's teeth are not constantly naturally filed down, they become long and sharp. This can firstly cause mouth abscesses, that if left untreated can cause your dwarf hamster to become very sick and even die if the infection spreads. Secondly, overgrown teeth can prevent the dwarf hamster from putting food into its mouth; left unaddressed the dwarf hamster will die of starvation.

Unpainted, untreated blocks of wood are best for your dwarf hamster to keep its teeth well filed down. It is best to buy wood from pet stores and online pet accessory retailers that confirm that they are suitable for dwarf hamsters. Don't use dry wood picked up from your garden or anywhere else because it could house parasites and also contain toxins absorbed from herbicides and pesticides.

Another option is to give your dwarf hamster hard dog biscuits, that are unflavoured, to chew on. Most dwarf hamsters enjoy chewing on the dog biscuits and a box will last you a very long time. Ensure that the biscuits are plain and contain no flavourings, as some flavouring agents can be harmful to your dwarf hamster.

It is recommended that you put a number of healthy, natural chews in your hamsters living environment so that it does not become bored and go back to chewing the cage bars.

Toys
- although not essential, the more stimulation your dwarf hamster has in its living environment, the happier it will be. Boredom in all pets can lead to behavioural problems and reparative behaviour patterns that are very destructive.

There are many commercially manufactured dwarf hamster toys available- most of them made of plastic. Because of the health hazards of potential toxic content, and the negative impact discarded plastic has on the environment, there is absolutely no need for you to buy plastic toys.

Wooden and cork toys are readily available online form pet accessory retailers and you can also make your own from unprinted cardboard boxes and toilet roll holders. Wooden popsicle sticks also make wonderful toys for dwarf hamsters. Remember to always use non-toxic glue when making your own dwarf hamster toys.

An Internet search will give you a host of step-by-step tutorials on how to build cardboard multi-story castles, bridges, popsicle-stick ladders, platforms and many more ideas to create a dwarf hamster paradise at very little cost.

Chapter 5: Day-to-Day Care of your Dwarf Hamster

Once you have set up your dwarf hamster's living environment and introduced your new dwarf hamster to its new home, you will have to give your dwarf hamster daily attention to ensure that it settles in, is eating regularly, moving around its new home and exploring. These are signs that you have selected a healthy dwarf hamster. The daily care does not end there though. Acquiring a dwarf hamster (or any pet) is a daily commitment to feed and take care of the dwarf hamster's needs for the duration of its life because all pets rely exclusively on their human parents for survival. You have to live up to this commitment every day.

Settling In

You have to allow your new dwarf hamster some time to settle in to its new living environment. Your dwarf hamster will be experiencing new smells, new sounds, a new habitat and possibly a new diet. All of this can be quite overwhelming for the small little animal and it may feel quite scared and insecure, leading it to spend more time hiding in its hamster-house, which provides a sense of safety and comfort. If your dwarf hamster has not had much human contact previously, it may be a bit wild which will add to its sense of fear. None of this is a problem if you allow yourself to understand the situation and don't have unrealistic expectations.

Allow your new dwarf hamster to settle in by changing the water and replenishing food without making any attempt to approach it. When your dwarf hamster is out and about, observe from a distance. The living environment must be cleaned out at least once a week; do it gently as well without disturbing your new dwarf hamster. Always ensure that you wash your hands thoroughly before and after cleaning. While you are cleaning, speak gently to your dwarf hamster, even if you can't see it. In this way it gets used to the sound of your voice, which is important because not all dwarf hamsters have good eyesight.

Because at this stage you will not have much direct contact with your dwarf hamster, and it may scurry into its hamster-house when you approach. While cleaning out look for any signs of diarrhoea which is an indication that your dwarf hamster is sick and needs veterinary care, or blood which could indicate an injury.

In this way you are introducing your smell to your dwarf hamster and also giving reassurance that there is nothing to be feared. Don't try to coax your new dwarf hamster with food in the first few days; wait until you can see that it is becoming settled. Also don't try to catch or grab at your new dwarf hamster because that could leave you with a good bite, and leave your dwarf hamster more fearful. Easy does it – give it time!

Taming

Dwarf hamsters that have had very little human contact previously, especially dwarf hamsters that have come from commercial breeders who produce pups en-masse without much care or interaction, could be quite wild when you acquire them. Taming this type of dwarf hamster will require time and patience because you need to win over its trust and that will be a gradual process.

If your new dwarf hamster has been bred by a smaller breeder who has a genuine interest in the little rodents, it could be quite accustomed to human contact and will therefore be easier to tame. Breeders who have a genuine interest will care about the pup's well being. The pups would previously have been picked up and handled by humans to ensure that they are healthy, and they may even have been played with. In this instance, winning over your dwarf hamster's trust will just be a matter of it becoming accustomed to your smell and its new living environment.

The species of dwarf hamster that you have acquired will also play a role in how easy it will be for you to tame your dwarf hamster. Russian Winter Whites are naturally quite relaxed and enjoy being handled and played with. Campbell's male and females have a strong territorial instinct and can resist your hands intruding into their living environment. They can bite, so it is best that they are lifted with a receptacle like a mug or ladle. Once out of their living environment their territorial instinct dissipates and they are quite happy to be handled and played with.

Always use the same receptacle and your dwarf hamster will come to recognise it, happily jumping is for play-time. Roborovski's are more of an observe-but-don't touch species and do not like being handled and played with. You can, over much time, train your Roborovski to climb onto your hand and then up your arm and explore around your body, and when done you can put it back into its living environment by gently slanting your arm into its living environment and let it climb down again. Roborovski's startle easily and any sudden movement can cause it jump and run.

All dwarf hamsters are very small and very fast little animals, with the Roborovski's being incredibly fast, so all play should be in an enclosed are, away from other pets and without any escape routes.

If you have acquired a hybrid dwarf hamster its temperament can be quire unpredictable and you will have to approach taming carefully, observing its reaction and behaviour towards your touch and handling it accordingly.

Once you are sure that your dwarf hamster has settled into its new living environment you can begin to gently approach it. Always wash your hands thoroughly before putting them into your dwarf hamsters living environment and handling your dwarf hamster. Also wash your hands thoroughly afterwards.

It is best to begin training your dwarf hamster when it is naturally active, which is in the evening because they are nocturnal. If you wake your dwarf hamster during the day, your taming exercise will be getting off to a bad start. Begin by slowly lowering your hand into your dwarf hamsters living environment and speaking to it softly and see how it reacts. By now it should be used to your smell and voice. If your dwarf hamster tolerates your hand but does not approach it, let it be; keep your hand in the cage for a while and then slowly withdraw it. Stay around the enclosure while your dwarf hamster goes about doing dwarf hamster-things. Continue to speak softly to it every now and then. You can try lowering your hand into the enclosure again after a while; if your dwarf hamster still does not approach but stays outside of its hamster-house, you are making progress. Don't try to coax or grab your dwarf hamster because that will undo your progress made.

Continue in this way for a day or two, and if your dwarf hamster does not approach you (remember they are very curious little animals), then very slowly begin to move your hand towards your dwarf hamster while speaking softly and see how it reacts. You may find at this stage that your dwarf hamster is quite receptive and stays where it is. Hold your hand still and see if it moves towards you and begins to smell your hand. If it does, you've made further progress! Still don't try to coax it or grab at it because that will undo your progress.

If you continue at this rate and your dwarf hamster continues reacting positively, you can move on to gently stroking it. If it is receptive to your touch, you will probably be able to gently lift it up and let it sit in your cupped hands for a while for reassurance. Once you have reached this stage you can safely begin to handle and play with your dwarf hamster and it will most likely respond very well, eventually jumping into your hands for much loved play-time!

If your dwarf hamster scurries away when you lower your hand into its living environment and does not become accustomed to your hand, try introducing a receptacle like a mug or a ladle. Keep your hand on the receptacle. Always speak gently to your dwarf hamster. Eventually, curiosity will get the better of your dwarf hamster and it will come over to investigate the receptacle. If your dwarf hamster is investigating, but still skittish, don't make any attempt to lift it out. Continue with this routine for a few days and your dwarf hamster's further curiosity will probably lead it to jump into the receptacle. At that stage you can slowly lift the receptacle and pass the dwarf hamster from the receptacle to your cupped hands. If your dwarf hamster prefers a receptacle, it is probably due its territorial instincts.

Once your dwarf hamster is comfortable to be out of its living environment, keep it out for five or ten minutes to start off with so that it does not startle. You can extend play-time over time once your dwarf hamster is comfortable in your presence and unlikely to startle.
Your hamster may nibble at your hands. That is not a bite; that is how dwarf hamsters explore. Once you have tamed your dwarf hamster your job is not done. You have to play with your dwarf hamster every day to keep it healthy and tame. If you stop lifting your dwarf hamster up for play-time for even a few days, you could find it becoming fearful again. If you stop for any length of time, your dwarf hamster will probably have to be tamed all over again.

Water

It is vital that you check the water level everyday and ensure that your dwarf hamster is never left without access to clean water. Also check the water spout every day to ensure that it is not blocked. Water should be changed daily, irrespective of the water level in the bottle. The water bottle must be sanitised at least once a week to discourage the build-up of slime and ensure that bacteria does not build up in the bottle and spout. Sanitise the inside of the water bottle with a weak bleach dilution of 1 part bleach to 32 parts water, or a dilution 1 part distilled white vinegar, 1 part salt and 4 parts boiling water. Rinse the water bottle thoroughly with either solution, and then rinse again with clean boiled water to ensure that all traces of bleach or vinegar and salt have been removed from the bottle. Also sanitise the drinking spout in the same manner.

Avoid giving your dwarf hamster chlorinated water and water that may contain heavy metals. Not all water filtration systems remove all chlorine and heavy metals from tap water. Untreated tap water is not recommended for your dwarf hamster. De-chlorinating tap water is an option as is unflavoured bottled water. If you want to de-chlorinate tap water you can readily buy a de-chlorinator form pet stores that sell fish and aquarium equipment. Never use distilled water because it has been processed to remove all mineral components, many of which are vital for normal body functions. A cheaper and convenient option is to boil water and then leave it in an open container for about forty eight hours before filling your dwarf hamster's water bottle.

Food

Although dwarf hamsters are omnivorous, in the wild their diet comprises primarily of seeds, dried fruit, parts of plants and to a much lesser extent, insects.

In captivity a balanced diet for a dwarf hamster should be made up of 60% to 65% carbohydrates, 16% to 24 % protein and 5% to 7% fat. Quality commercially produced dwarf hamster food can give your dwarf hamster all the nutrition required to stay healthy. The most important factor of quality commercially produced food is that the mix of dry grains, nuts and seeds must be well balanced with no one particular component dominating the content. If your dwarf hamster does not eat a balanced mix of grains, nuts and seeds, it can lead to digestive problems, weight gain and nutritional deficiencies. Some commercial producers include small amounts of protein in their mix, like dried meal-worm.

Commercial dwarf hamster food comes in a mixture of seeds only, seeds mixed with insect protein, seeds mixed with dried fruits and leaves, seeds mixed with pellets and pellets only. Most claim to be fortified with vitamins and minerals as well. Always choose to buy the best quality dwarf hamster food that you can afford. Dwarf hamsters will not all eat exactly the same food. Not only are they different species that originate from a different geographical area, but many will have their own personal taste like many other pets can have. Some dwarf hamsters do not like pellets and it is not recommended that your dwarf hamster has a diet comprising of pellets only. The value of pellets is that they have to be gnawed at, and that aids in keeping your dwarf hamsters teeth worn down. There are also blocks of dwarf hamster food available that are excellent for gnawing on.

Apart from commercially produced food, there are also other foods that you can safely feed your dwarf hamster and others that must be completely avoided as they can cause sickness and even death. Fresh fruit and vegetables must be a very occasional treat, as they can lead to diarrhoea and death. Dwarf hamsters originate from very cold climates and desert areas where fresh vegetables and fruits are not readily available, so their digestives systems are not adapted for fresh produce.

Your dwarf hamster's food should be put in a sturdy food dish that cannot be tipped over (and preferably not made of plastic). Some dwarf hamsters like to sit in their food bowl while eating and fresh treats should not be mixed with seeds or pellets in the food bowl because the dry food can become damp and contaminated. Instead, hide treats as well as dry food and pellets all around the living environment to provide your dwarf hamster with stimulation similar to foraging in the wild.

Give your dwarf hamster about a tablespoon of food a day. Remember that they have cheek pouches, so an empty food bowl is not an indication of a hungry dwarf hamster. They instinctively will store uneaten food in their cheek pouches and store it in their hamster-house to nibble on in between periods of sleep. Because dwarf hamsters are nocturnal, it is best to fill their food dish in the evening. Remove any food from the living environment that has been wet or contaminated everyday to prevent the growth of bacteria or fungus.

Over feeding your dwarf hamster can result in weight gain and health problems related to obesity.

Commercially produced grain, nut and seed treats are available that you can be suspended in your dwarf hamster's living environment, but you can also make treats for your dwarf hamster. Small seeds combined with water and baked in an oven can be threaded on to a piece on natural string, free of dyes or bleach for a quick, inexpensive treat that will keep your dwarf hamster entertained for days. An Internet search will give you a host of step-by-step recipes.

Foods That Must Not Be Fed

Listed below are foods that must not be given to your dwarf hamster. If you want to introduce a new treat to your dwarf hamster, first conduct some research to see if it is suitable. Bad foods include:
- Human junk food like pizza, chocolate, cake, etc
- Anything sticky that can become stuck in cheek pouches, like peanut butter, jam fruit gums, etc
- Anything sharp that can cut the cheek pouches inside, like potato crisps, hard boiled candy, etc
- All processed food like cheese, mayonnaise, hot-dog sausage, etc
- Alcohol, coffee, tea, fruit juice and soft drinks
- Salted or candied seeds and nuts
- All citrus fruits
- Onions and garlic
- Kidney beans
- Bitter almonds
- Avocado
- Potato
- Tomato
- Eggplant
- Fruit seeds

Foods That Can Be Fed

Listed below are foods that can be given to your dwarf hamster. If you want to introduce any of these as a new treat to your dwarf hamster, first give a very small amount and wait for at least twenty four hours to ensure that there is no allergy or negative reaction before giving any more. Good foods include:
- Asparagus
- Basil
- Bean sprouts
- Bell pepper
- Broccoli

- Carrot
- Corn
- Cucumber
- Green bean
- Kale
- Spinach
- Watercress
- Endive
- Parsnip
- Turnip
- Dandelion leaves
- Wheatgrass
- Brown rice pasta
- Boiled egg
- Mealworm
- Grasshopper
- Crickets
- Boiled plain salmon (no salt)
- Boiled plain chicken (no slat)

There are other foods that are safe to feed to your dwarf hamster. If you are unsure, always err on the side of caution by doing some Internet research before you introduce something new. It is very important to ensure that you feed the above foods to your dwarf hamster in very small amounts, and only occasionally.

Cleaning and Hygiene

Your dwarf hamster's living environment must be kept clean and hygienic to preserve your dwarf hamster's health and your own. You must always wash your hands thoroughly before putting them into the living environment for any reason, and after you are done.

You must replenish food and water daily and remove any bits of food, substrate or nesting material that has become soiled or contaminated. Mouldy food, substrate and nesting material can become a breeding ground for bacteria and fungus, endangering the health of your dwarf hamster as well as your own and any other family and pets.

If any area in the living environment has become wet, for example from a leaking water bottle, it must be immediately cleaned of all wet substrate, nesting material and any toys or treats in the area. The area must be thoroughly dried and substrate and bedding replaced with dry material. Dwarf hamsters should never get wet because if they do it will lead to sickness and possibly death.

The entire living environment must be thoroughly cleaned out every week. Gently place your dwarf hamster in a small safe receptacle and empty the living environment of all accessories, toys, food, substrate, nesting material, etc. Wipe down all accessories, toys, food dishes and water bottles. Discard substrate, nesting material and sand. Sanitise the entire living area, inside and out as well as all accessories, food dishes and water bottles with a weak bleach dilution of 1 part bleach to 32 parts water, or a dilution 1 part distilled white vinegar, 1 part salt and 4 parts boiling water. Wipe everything down thoroughly with either solution and then wipe down again with clean boiled water to ensure that all traces of bleach or vinegar and salt have been removed. Wait for everything to dry out completely before you put in new substrate, nesting material, sand, food and water.

Once all is done, gently return your dwarf hamster to its sparkling clean living environment.

Chapter 6: Dwarf Hamster Body Language

Like all animals, dwarf hamsters communicate with each other and will begin to communicate with you once they have settled and if you pay them daily attention.

Obviously dwarf hamsters don't speak, but there are many cues that you can pick up from its body language once you get to know it well. Dwarf hamsters also have their own personalities like animals do. Some are more reserved, others more outgoing, some very loving and others more independent. It can be a wonderfully rewarding journey getting to know your new little pet.

Amongst other dwarf hamsters a lot of communication is conveyed by smell. By sniffing at each others' scent glands they can identify each other, sense sickness and even read their mood. As a human parent to a dwarf hamster your sense of smell is not really going to get you far, but your dwarf hamster will definitely get to know you by your scent. That is another reason why it is vital to wash your hands before you put them into your dwarf hamster's cage. If your hands are contaminated with a foreign smell it may not recognise you and feel threatened.

Reading Body Language
A happy, healthy dwarf hamster that feels safe and content will be at ease in your company once it has settled in. Here are some of the more common messages, signals and emotions your dwarf hamster will give to you as you interact and get to know each other. Remember though that because all animals have some individual personality traits you may pick up some others, maybe unique to your dwarf hamster.

- Half-open eyes and ears laid back says - "I'm still sleepy; give me a few more minutes!" or "What's up!"

- Yawning and / or stretching says -"Hello, I feel great and have just had a good sleep!"
- Sitting straight up with ears forward says - "I see something that I like!"
- Running interspersed with grooming says - "I'm excited, agitated or confused!"
- Squeaking when lifted from living environment says - "I'm unhappy; put me back!" or "I don't feel well!"
- Grooming says - "I'm happy and need to clean up after napping!" or "I'm happy and need to clean up after playtime!"
- Burrowing in substrate says - "I'm a happy dwarf hamster, playing around and looking for snacks!"
- Startled when you approach says - "You caught me unaware!" or "I'm not settled enough yet!"
- Standing on its hind legs with front paws ready to swat at you says -"I feel threatened; back off!"
- Ears forward, cheek pouches puffed and mouth open says - "I'm frightened!"
- Sudden empting check pouches says - "Fight or flight; I'm ready for flight!"
- Turning on its back and showing incisors says - "I'm very frightened; I will attack!"
- Flattening its body and creeping slowly forward says - "I'm out of my comfort zone and trying to become invisible!"
- It freezes on the spot says -"I'm afraid and I hope you'll think I'm dead!"
- If your dwarf hamster is always hiding says - "Consider where you've placed my living environment! Maybe the environment is too noisy or children are allowed access to me!"
- Your dwarf hamster does not respond when you approach says - "Help, I don't feel well or I'm injured!"

- Your dwarf hamster greets you but is lethargic says - "Help, I don't feel well or I'm injured!" or "My living environment is overheated!"
- Your dwarf hamster bites you immediately you put your hand in its living environment says - "I don't know you well enough yet. You still scare me; give me more time!"
- Your dwarf hamster shows you no interest but continues with repetitive behaviour says - "I'm going crazy in this little cage with no stimulation. Please buy me a bigger and better equipped home!"

If your dwarf hamster shows aggression or fear when you put your hand into its living environment it could need more time to settle in. If you believe that is should be settled, it could be defending its territory so try lifting it out of its living environment with a receptacle like a mug or a ladle. That should address territorial behaviour. If it continues to display signs of fear like squeaking or hissing, it may need more time to adjust.

Other problems that can cause your dwarf hamster not to settle is that you have not placed its living environment is a suitable place, children and other pets may be harassing the dwarf hamster in your absence or it could be sick. Genetic mental issues cannot be ruled out if it is a hybrid. Do some Internet research, join groups of dwarf hamster owners online and ask experts in dwarf hamster husbandry for advice. Most people who join this type of group are genuine small animal lovers and will be more than willing to give you information, tips and advice.

Chapter 7: Dwarf Hamster Fighting

If you have acquired a pair of dwarf hamsters or a small group, the chances of fighting are very real, particularly if they are of mixed sex. Males are territorial and some females are too! If the living environment is not big enough to allow each of them their own territory (and that includes their own hamster-home, exercise wheel, food bowl, etc) fighting will be inevitable. Many times territorial fights can be to the death.

Although many female dwarf hamsters can coexist happily in pairs or small communities if all acquired and introduced to each other at a very young age, it is not always successful and fights can break out over territory, or if the living environment is crowded.

Females in the late stages of gestation will also become aggressive to any other dwarf hamsters, male or female - and will display aggressive behaviour towards you as well, particularly once her pups have been born and for the next two weeks thereafter.

Remember that in the wild dwarf hamsters live in wide territorial ranges, and although they may live in communities there are numerous burrows and many tunnels that each community shares. In short - dwarf hamsters need space, despite being so tiny!

As a pet to novice human parents, a single dwarf hamster in a well equipped living environment is by far the best option. The trauma of watching dwarf hamsters fight is not something that you want to witness or allow your family to witness either.

Cues and Body Language that Precede Fighting
You can observe impending aggression in dwarf hamsters, and as you are responsible for their wellbeing it is important to get to know

your dwarf hamsters and become familiar with their body language and displays of emotion. If you can see that two dwarf hamsters are getting in one another's way you can separate them before the situation escalates and fighting breaks out to prevent a potential tragedy.

Circling each other and pushing at one-another's abdomen could be an attempt to establish the sex of the other or smell the scent glands. It can look quite aggressive, but it can just be over eager attempts to get to know each other. This behaviour should however not continue and should be a once-off because once they have established what they want to know there would be no need for circling and pushing. If it continues it could be a sign that they are testing their strength against each other. Keep a close eye on the pair!

Wrestling among male pups is a test of strength, but it is not advised that two males be housed in the same living environment. If you find your dwarf hamsters (female or male) rising up on to its hind legs with mouth open and cheek pouches puffed up, extending its front limbs towards another dwarf hamster, this is a definite sign that it trying to ward off an aggressor. If one of the dwarf hamsters does not want to fight, it will submit by extending its paw to the aggressor, flick its tail and avoid eye contact. This is in effect surrender. You still need to keep a close eye on the pair because the aggressor may begin to bully the subordinate dwarf hamster, especially in an overcrowded environment.

Where neither of the dwarf hamsters is willing to surrender, a wrestling match will ensue. It begins from an upright stance and one will lunge at the other trying to bite the underbelly. The two dwarf hamsters will then begin to roll around, each trying to get the better of the other. If one accepts defeat during the fight it will lie on its back and freeze in this position. At this point the fight is over, but you still need to keep a close eye on the pair because the aggressor may begin to bully the subordinate dwarf hamster, especially in an overcrowded environment.

If neither dwarf hamster is willing to surrender, the wrestling match will become more aggressive, vocal and physical. Biting becomes more serious and the dwarf hamsters will begin to draw blood. They can inflict life threatening wounds on each other. At this stage, even if one surrenders and runs for cover, the aggressor can chase it and continue attacking it. If there is no escape, the aggressor could kill it.

Obviously you need to intervene as soon as you see an aggressive fight break out. Don't try to separate them with your bare hands. Try squirting them with cold water from a syringe or something similar to briefly separate them and then lift either one of them out of the living environment using a mug or gloves and place it in a separate living space. Check both the fighting dwarf hamsters for signs of bleeding and potential lacerations. If there is excessive bleeding or lacerations you may need to seek immediate veterinary care for one or both.

You need to carefully analyse what caused the aggression and fighting. There is a small change that you can at a later stage try to re-introduce the two dwarf hamsters but it is unlikely that they will get along and coexist peacefully in the long run.

Dwarf hamsters, both male and female, thrive well living a solitary life as long as their living environment is spacious and they are provided with accessories to provide stimulation.

Chapter 8: Health and Veterinary Care

Dwarf hamsters are very small, fragile animals and even the smallest of injuries can lead to death. You must pay careful attention to your dwarf hamster daily if you want to keep it healthy. It is important that you ensure that your local veterinarian practice does treat small animals like dwarf hamsters, and if they do not that you identify the closest veterinarian practice that does so that you don't waste valuable time in the case of an emergency. You can conduct an Internet search to find your local board of veterinary practitioners and their website will either list registered veterinarians who are qualified and registered to treat dwarf hamsters, or you could call them to confirm. Dwarf hamsters are considered to be Exotic Mammals and require specialised veterinary treatment. Not all veterinary practices are equipped to treat them.

If there is no veterinarian that treats dwarf hamsters in your area, you should carefully consider acquiring a dwarf hamster as a pet. Dwarf hamsters, like all other pets and humans get injured or get sick and require medical attention. If you know that you are unable to provide qualified veterinary care for a dwarf hamster it would be very irresponsible to acquire one as a pet. Home treatments that can safely be used to treat cats and dogs can be toxic to such a small animal. Even topical antiseptics, ointments or balms could prove fatal to a dwarf hamster if applied. Think responsibly – no qualified vet; no dwarf hamster as a pet!

Daily health hazards to your dwarf hamster are leg and paw injuries from unsuitable exercise wheels or getting caught up in fibres from unsuitable nesting material. Cuts to cheek pouches or the mouth can be sustained from gnawing on plastic accessories. Diarrhoea can be caused by an unsuitable diet, or bacterial infection. These situations would all require veterinary treatment if you want your dwarf hamster to survive. Medicating and treating your dwarf hamster yourself is not advised.

Dwarf hamsters are also prone to other diseases and it is vital that you remain vigilant of signs of illness, which could include lethargy, loss of appetite, skin lesions or patches of hair loss, dull eyes and diarrhoea, bleeding from anywhere, including blood in the urine, compulsive behaviour patterns amongst others. All of these symptoms require veterinary treatment. With a small animal like a dwarf hamster it is not advised to wait to see if the symptoms pass or to try to treat the condition yourself. Because of their very small size, even a slight overdose of medication could be fatal. Some of the diseases that dwarf hamsters can suffer from are broad and include:

Abscesses
- are infected pockets of pus that form in the skin tissue resulting in a painful bulge under the skin on any area of the body, limbs, cheek pouches or the mouth. You may become aware of the bulge while playing with your dwarf hamster, it may obviously visible or you may notice soiling on your dwarf hamster's coat if the abscess has ruptured, spilling puss and blood. They are caused by bacterial infection and generally result from an untreated injury. You may also notice swelling around your dwarf hamster's cheeks and neck because the lymph nodes become swollen if the infection is severe. Abscesses require immediate veterinary treatment to prevent the spread of bacteria.

Tissue samples need to be taken from the abscess to confirm that it is not other common skin conditions, such as cysts and hematomas. Depending on the diagnosis, your veterinarian will either lance and drain the abscess and then flush it with an antiseptic solution or opt to remove it surgically.
If your dwarf hamster does undergo surgery to remove the abscess, you must ensure that it does not groom the operation wound, as this will interfere with the healing process. Also follow all medical

advice given by your veterinarian with regards to cleaning and dressing the wound until it is healed.

Dwarf hamsters can also develop abscesses from impacted cheek pouches. Captive dwarf hamsters are inclined to impacted cheek pouches caused by nesting material or substrate being taken in with food. If you notice that your dwarf hamster's cheek pouches remain full, the pouches could be impacted. If impacted pouches are not emptied, abscesses can form and your dwarf hamster could become very sick. Impacted cheek pouches can also lead to starvation. If your dwarf hamster still seems healthy, the impaction may not yet have caused any damage and you can try emptying the check pouches yourself.

Dwarf hamsters empty their check pouches by using their two front paws to push the food forward and out of their mouth. You can try firm but gentle strokes with your finger along the outside coat of the pouch or both pouches towards the mouth to try to dislodge the impacted food and other matter. If that is unsuccessful, you can try opening your dwarf hamster's mouth to physically access the compacted food and remove it. This must be done very carefully using something like a wooden orange stick (used for manicures) wrapped well in crepe bandage and soaked in pre-boiled water to ensure that you do not cut the inside if the pouches, leave behind fibres or introduce bacteria. You can also try loosening the compacted food by flushing the cheek pouch or pouches with pre-boiled and cooled water dropped into the pouch or pouches.

If you notice any blood or pus coming from the pouch or pouches while trying any of the above methods, stop immediately and take your dwarf hamster to a veterinarian, as there may already be an infection or even an abscess present in the skin.

If you are not able to remove the compacted food form your dwarf hamster's cheek pouch or pouches, take it to a veterinarian for professional medical help.

Once you have identified what caused your dwarf hamster's cheek pouch or pouches to compact, remove those items from the living enclosure or eliminate those foods from its diet to prevent any reoccurrence of the problem.

More rarely, dwarf hamsters can develop cheek pouch eversion. This is when the cheek pouch actually turns inside-out and the dwarf hamster is unable to correct it by itself. You can correct the cheek pouch by using a small, blunt object. If a cheek pouch is everted over a period of time without being noticed it can become inflamed, infected and septic, requiring surgical removal of the septic (necrotic) tissue. Untreated this can lead to death from sepsis.

Allergies

- affect dwarf hamsters just as easily as they do humans. As with humans, the catalyst of the allergic reaction can be difficult to pinpoint. If you introduce your dwarf hamster to new food, substrate or nesting material and you see any negative reaction, remove and avoid giving it to your dwarf hamster again. Symptoms of allergy include dry skin, hair loss, diarrhoea, sneezing, itchy eyes, wheezing skin irritation, swollen paws, inflammation on any area of the body and dry skin around the eyes, ears, nose and mouth.

Symptoms of allergy appear almost immediately after the allergen has been introduced to your dwarf hamster, so if your hamster has been with you for some time, immediately investigate what new things have been introduced to its living environment or to the area outside. If nothing in the environment has changed and the symptoms persist it is best to take your dwarf hamster to your veterinarian because it could be symptoms of infection rather than allergy.

Amyloidosis
- affects mainly older dwarf hamsters. It is a condition where the body begins to produce dense sheets of proteins called amyloid. The amyloid is then deposited throughout the dwarf hamster's body, including the vital organs. This prevents the vital organs (heart, liver and kidneys) from functioning normally and fluid retention begins to build up in the hamster's abdomen.

The first symptoms will be an enlarged abdomen, less urination and smaller faeces. Veterinary intervention is required to confirm the condition, however you will be advised that there is no cure for amyloidosis.

Cardiac Disease
- most commonly affects older dwarf hamsters, although it can be diagnosed in younger dwarf hamsters as well. Symptoms include shortness of breath, stopping all exercise, limited activity, depression and lethargy. If your veterinarian diagnosis cardiac disease you will be advised that there is no treatment for cardiac disease in dwarf hamsters.

Circling
- is a common term used for any compulsive behaviour like circling, rocking back and forth or twitching of the head. This is a condition where your dwarf hamster will begin constantly turning in a circular movement with its head turned toward its tail, rocking back and forth or twitching its head to one side, or from side to side without any apparent reason. Circling or twitching its head to one side can be a symptom that your dwarf hamster has developed an ear infection and has earache. A trip to your veterinarian will confirm this and an ear

infection can easily be treated with antibiotics.

Circling, rocking or twitching, as well as sitting motionless staring aimlessly could indicate a more severe problem related to brain injury or neurological dysfunction. Like humans, dwarf hamsters can also become affected by brain injury which could happen as a result of being dropped during play, getting its head caught in its living environment (for example between its exercise wheel and a wall), being temporarily starved of oxygen (for example chocking, having its head caught between cage bars or while being handled) or as a result of a genetic neurological condition, generally resulting from poor or unscrupulous breeding selection. If the compulsive circling, rocking, twitching or motionless staring is as a result of brain injury or a neurological genetic defect, it may be accompanied by aggression, which will make your dwarf hamster difficult to handle. If your dwarf hamster has suddenly become aggressive, don't ignore the behaviour change and keep away from it out of fear. Use a receptacle or wear thick gloves to remove your dwarf from its living environment and take it to your veterinarian. You assumed responsibility for your dwarf hamster's wellbeing when you acquired it. You must live up to responsible pet care!
Once again, your veterinarian must diagnose the cause of your dwarf hamster's compulsive behaviour, and it must be addressed. Even if your dwarf hamster looks healthy and feeds and drinks, which can be the case particularly with genetic neurological defects your dwarf hamster suffering! Although to some the compulsions may appear to be amusing antics, to your dwarf hamster it is trauma! Not taking your dwarf hamster to a veterinarian to diagnose compulsive behaviour is tantamount to animal cruelty.

Clonic Seizures
- is a genetic condition generally resulting from poor and unscrupulous breeding. Symptoms of a seizure are jerking limbs, uncontrollable body movement, an open mouth and possibly an

extended tongue with saliva drooling from the mouth. Involuntary urination and diarrhoea may occur. Moments before the onset of a seizure, your dwarf hamster may adopt a rigid stare and dull facial expression.

If your dwarf hamster has a seizure it is vital that you remain calm because there is nothing that you can do to stop a seizure once it has begun. Do not lift your dwarf hamster from its living environment, but rather very gently cup your hands around its sides and speak softly to it to calm and reassure it. Seizures are an extremely traumatic experience for animals and humans.

When the seizure has passed, leave your dwarf hamster to rest and recover. Don't try to feed it anything or give it water. It will return to normal after a short while and feed and drink at will again. If you have a dwarf hamster that is prone to seizures you will have to remove any accessories from its living environment that can be hazardous and cause injury during a seizure. If the dwarf hamster is one of a pair or part of a community, it is best to remove it to live on its own.

There is no cure for seizure not medication to control seizures in dwarf hamsters. Creating a safe living environment and providing your dwarf hamster with support and care will allow it to live a normal life.

Dehydration

– can very easily set-in if your dwarf hamster is exposed to a sudden increase in environmental temperature. This can be due to direct sunlight, a heater being used in the room where the dwarf hamster is housed, or very hot spells in the weather. You must consider seasonal changes and what effect they have on the room temperature that your dwarf hamster's living environment is housed in. A room that is warm in winter could become like an oven to a small animal in summer, just like the use of a heater in a room to keep humans and lager animals warm in winter could have a negative effect on your dwarf hamster.

If you notice that your dwarf hamster has become inactive and is breathing heavily, or even hyperventilating, it could be suffering from dehydration. Move it away from the source of heat immediately. If necessary, remove it from its cage or aquarium as metal, plastic and glass can retain heat. Place your dwarf hamster in a cool safe place and put down a small shallow container of water for it to drink from with little effort. When your dwarf hamster's body temperature has dropped and its living environment has cooled down, you can return it to its home, but be sure to place the living environment is a more suitable area so that you hamster does not become dehydrated again.

If the environmental temperature in the room where your dwarf hamster is housed is too high, your dwarf hamster can become dehydrated very quickly because of its small size. Even if it has access to a water bottle and water, it is the external temperature that leads to dehydration. If the dehydration is not noticed very soon, your dwarf hamster will easily succumb to the condition.

To prevent dehydration, carefully consider the effect that seasonal changes have on the room where your dwarf hamster is housed. If the room is affected by seasonal changes that will cause the room to become substantially hotter, make a note to move your dwarf hamsters living environment with the onset of changing seasons. Dehydration in dwarf hamsters can very quickly be fatal so if you don't consider seasonal temperature changes to the room, you could come home to discover that your dwarf hamster died a very unpleasant death.

Diabetes

- is a relatively common disease in dwarf hamsters, and although previously diagnosed predominantly in Campbell's, hybrid breeding has resulted in the predisposition to diabetes to be present throughout the pet dwarf hamster population.

It is caused by a lack of insulin production by the pancreas, or the failure of the cell-receptors in the body to respond the insulin. The role of insulin is directly related to the passing of glucose from blood cells via cell-receptors for energy to maintain body function. Diabetes causes glucose to be excreted through the urine and that causes dehydration, which in turn causes constant thirst followed by frequent urination.

Symptoms you will first notice is a constantly thirsty dwarf hamster drinking water very often, frequent urination and weight loss. As the condition worsens, your dwarf hamster will become vulnerable to infections, particularly of the urinary tract.

If you suspect your dwarf hamster may have diabetes, take it to your veterinarian to confirm the diagnosis. If your dwarf hamster is diagnosed with diabetes you will have to introduce a complete change of diet. Any infections that your dwarf hamster has as a result of the condition will be treated with antibiotics, but because of dwarf hamsters very small size, insulin treatment is dangerous, so best avoided.

Your dwarf hamster will have to be put on a strict high protein fibre and low fat diet. Ask your vet for nutritional advice and recommended brands. If your diabetic dwarf hamster is one of a pair or lives in a community, it is best to separate it to live on its own so that the diet can be strictly controlled.

You will need to monitor your dwarf hamster's glucose and ketone levels at least once a week. Your vet would already have given you the optimum levels. Test strips are available from most pharmacies as they are the same as those used by humans. To test the dwarf hamster's urine, hold the strip against its genitals wile applying gentle pressure to the abdomen. That should produce at least a drop of urine, which is enough to do the test.

Any changes in the glucose and ketone levels must be addressed by again adapting your dwarf hamster's diet. Your veterinarian may be able to offer some advice, but there are many groups and blog posts on the Internet that can guide you.

Eye Diseases

- dwarf hamsters can suffer from various eye diseases so it is important to inspect your dwarf hamster's eyes every day. If you do not clean your dwarf hamster's living environment regularly, a build-up of ammonia from urine can cause eye irritation and discharge.

If your dwarf hamster's eyes are swollen, inflamed or have a discharge it is always best to seek veterinary advice rather than to self diagnose and medicate. Even if your dwarf hamster has an object stuck in its eye that it can't get rid of, take it to a veterinarian who has the right equipment to solve the problem rather than you dig in dwarf hamster's eye. Eyes are very sensitive and delicate.

Apart from general injuries and irritants that can cause your dwarf hamster's eyes to become inflamed and painful, dwarf hamsters can also suffer from specific eye diseases that can be diagnosed by your veterinarian.

Cataracts

- are another disease that can be present in older dwarf hamsters in particular. It can also occur in younger dwarf hamsters that have diabetes. It will begin as a mild cloudiness in the eyes and progress to a complete opaqueness and is a progressive condition that can eventually lead to total blindness. Cataracts do not cause any pain or discomfort. There is no treatment or cure for cataracts in dwarf hamsters, but again with quality care and support your dwarf hamster can live a healthy and quality life as many dwarf hamsters have very poor eye sight anyway.

Conjunctivitis
- commonly known as Pink Eye, is also an eye disease that can be contracted by dwarf hamsters. It can be caused by both bacteria and viruses. If it is a viral infection, the eye discharge will be accompanied by respiratory infection. Bacterial conjunctivitis will present with eye discharge, sneezing, wheezing and lethargy. It is best to consult your veterinarian as soon as possible to prevent either infection spreading the through your dwarf hamster's respiratory system. Bacterial infections can deteriorate very quickly into pneumonia, and that can cause your dwarf hamster to die.

Bacterial and viral infections like conjunctivitis are spread through outside conditions so it is vital that you keep your dwarf hamster's living environment clean and regularly sanitised. Washing your hands thoroughly before and after cleaning your dwarf hamsters living environment is vital, as it is when handling and playing with your dwarf hamster to prevent cross-contamination.

Entropion
- is a genetic condition in dwarf hamsters that causes the upper eyelid on one or both eyes to invert, resulting in the eyelashes and even fur to rub against the eyeball and cause irritation and inflammation. It does require veterinary intervention and the inflammation can be treated with antibiotic eye-drops to prevent infection. If the entropion is not severe you can very gently lift your dwarf hamster's eyelid and carefully brush the eyelashes and fur out

of the eye towards the outside. This can bring some temporary relief and would have to be a daily routine to have lasting results. If it is severe, the constant friction against the eyeball can cause a corneal ulcer that will result in blindness. In some cases the only option is to surgically remove the eye. In dwarf hamsters it is very difficult to correct the inversion surgically as can be done in many bigger animals like dogs because the dwarf hamster's eyelid is so small. This type of microsurgery is not deemed to be worth the risk because there is only a 50% chance that the eyelid will not invert again after a few months. If surgical removal of the eyeball is recommended to prevent recurring eye infections, it will not negatively affect your dwarf hamster very badly, as many dwarf hamsters have poor eyesight. With quality care and support from its human parent, your dwarf hamster can live a healthy and quality life.

Glaucoma
- is a build-up of pressure inside the eye. It is most commonly found in Campbell's and Russian Winter White's. Symptoms include enlarged bulging eyes that become dry. Glaucoma can also cause an eye to rupture. A veterinarian will be able to make a definite diagnosis and advise you on whether they eye should be surgically removed, or if it can be treated with medicated eye drops. If you support your dwarf hamster and provide quality care, it can live a healthy and quality life as many dwarf hamsters have very poor eye sight anyway. Glaucoma is a genetic condition, so dwarf hamsters with glaucoma should not be bred.

Microphthalmia
- is another genetic condition that is found in dwarf hamsters and it can affect either one (unilateral microphthalmia) or both eyes (bilateral microphthalmia). It results in the dwarf hamster being born with very small or no eyes at all. Even if born with small eyes, the dwarf hamster will probably be blind. This condition will be evident

when you first see the dwarf hamster, but with quality care and support your dwarf hamster can live a healthy and quality life.

Sticky-Eye
- is a condition that affects older dwarf hamsters, but can affect younger dwarf hamsters as well. It is caused by eye secretions while your dwarf hamster is sleeping. These secretions are normal to keep the eyes moist, but if there is too much secretion it flows out of the closed eyes and dries out, sticking the lower and upper eyelid together. Your dwarf hamster will be unable to open its eye when it wakes up. In the immediate term you can gently apply a lukewarm wet cloth to your dwarf hamster's eyes to dissolve the dried secretion, but a visit to your veterinarian is advised to ensure that it is definitely sticky-eye and not a bacterial or viral eye infection.

Gastrointestinal
- infections and diseases can affect your dwarf hamster at any time. To ensure that you pick up any infections as quickly as possible, inspect your dwarf hamster's faeces every day when you are spot cleaning your dwarf hamster's living environment. Healthy dwarf hamster faeces are rice-shaped, almost black in colour and very dry. Don't be alarmed if you find your dwarf hamster eating its faeces because it is very normal and allows it to ingest B vitamins produced by micro-flora.

Constipation
- is compaction of the faeces. Symptoms of constipation include an arched back, swollen abdomen, protruding anus and no, or far less than normal visible faeces. It is caused by dehydration due to your dwarf hamster not drinking enough water. Always ensure that your dwarf hamster has access to clean, fresh water, and if your dwarf hamster is drinking from a water bottle ensure that the spout has not become blocked. Lack of exercise and parasites can also cause constipation. Young pups can become constipated if they cannot

reach their water supply; ensure that the water is placed within reach of small pups.

If your dwarf hamster has access to clean, fresh water and exercises regularly, and is still constipated, it is best to seek veterinary advice because your dwarf hamster could have a bowel obstruction that can eventually cause the bowl to become septic and lead to death. Laxative treatment for constipation is best administered under veterinary instruction.

Diarrhoea
- is a dangerous condition in all small animals because they can easily succumb to dehydration. It can easily be identified if your dwarf hamster's faeces have become loose, runny or watery, sometimes with traces of blood. A common cause of loose faeces is a change in diet, or being fed too many fresh treats - especially foods like cucumber, celery or lettuce that have a very high water content. If you are feeding your dwarf hamster fresh treats and you notice that it is passing loose faeces, cut back on the treats and feed dry food only for a few days until the loose faeces abate and return to normal.

If your dwarf hamster has been on antibiotic treatment for any condition anywhere up to two weeks previously, your dwarf hamster could have developed an overgrowth of gut-flora. Take your dwarf hamster back to the veterinarian for confirmation and the administration of probiotic supplements.

Tyzzer's disease
- is a contagious disease that can be passed on to other dwarf hamsters and any rodents. Early symptoms are very watery, yellow diarrhoea together with lethargy and dehydration. The disease is severe, and in some cases your dwarf hamster could die before you become fully aware of the symptoms. Tyzzer's disease very quickly

spreads to the heart, liver and through the intestines. Your veterinarian may try fluid and antibiotic administration, but the prognosis is very poor and treatment unsuccessful.

If your dwarf hamster has been diagnosed with Tyzzer's disease, the living environment should be emptied of all contents. All substrate, nesting material and food must be discarded and other items and well as the entire cage or tank must be thoroughly disinfected with a strong antiseptic solution and boiling water. The living environment and accessories should be left open in a room where it will stand in direct sunlight and not be used again for a few months. Before introducing your dwarf hamster, if it did recover, or a new dwarf hamster to the living environment again it should be washed out again and sanitised with a weak bleach dilution of 1 part bleach to 32 parts water to prevent re-infection.

Salmonella and E.Coli
- can be contracted by dwarf hamsters as well as other infectious diseases that affect the gastrointestinal tract. Salmonella and E.Coli can both initially briefly present with diarrhoea, but will very quickly show symptoms like lethargy, loss of appetite a dullness of expression and the eyes. Treatment in dwarf hamsters is seldom successful, so the prognosis is poor.

It is very important to note that these diseases can be spread to humans. Extreme hygiene measures are required, and you should wear protective gloves when clearing your dwarf hamsters living environment and cleaning it out. Again all substrate, nesting material and food must be discarded and other items and well as the entire cage or tank must be thoroughly disinfected with a strong antiseptic solution and boiling water. Once you have done this, discard the protective gloves and change and wash your clothes. The living environment and accessories should be left open in a room where it will stand in direct sunlight and not be used again for a few months.

Before introducing your dwarf hamster if it did recover or a new dwarf hamster to the living environment again it should be washed out again and sanitised with a weak bleach dilution of 1 part bleach to 32 parts water to prevent re-infection.

Greasy coat

- if you notice that your dwarf hamster's coat is unkempt and greasy it could be a symptom of sickness. Dwarf hamsters practice daily hygiene grooming their coats to get rid of any debris caught up in the hair, to remove excess oils and to spread newly produced oils through their coat.

If your dwarf hamster has stopped grooming, it is a symptom of lethargy. Effectively your dwarf hamster is too tired to groom itself. Never attempt to wash your dwarf hamster with water. It is probably already very ill, and wetting its coat will cause a respiratory infection over and above what is ailing it. It is a common symptom in older dwarf hamsters of cardiac or other diseases. A trip to your veterinarian will give you a diagnosis.

Nails

- that become overgrown can cause your dwarf hamster difficulty when running and climbing. It occurs when there are not enough rough surfaces in your dwarf hamster's living environment to naturally file its nails down. Your dwarf hamster's nails have become overgrown when you can see that they have formed a strong curve that turns inward towards the paw. The nails need to be trimmed, but it is best to have it done by your veterinarian because dwarf hamsters have blood vessels that carry down from their toes to the nail bed. If these blood vessels are cut it will cause your dwarf hamster extreme pain! If overgrown nails becomes a recurring problem you can ask your veterinarian to show you how to safely cut your dwarf hamsters nails and provide you with the right equipment to do so.

Parasites
- can infect all living creatures including dwarf hamsters. Any parasitic infection is very uncomfortable at the least, can cause sickness and can be deadly at the worst so parasitic infections must never be ignored. Parasites can transfer between dwarf hamsters, other pets and humans so always practice extreme hygiene if your dwarf hamster is diagnosed with a parasite infection. If the dwarf hamster diagnosed is one of a pair or part of a group, have the other dwarf hamsters checked as well to insure that they do not also have a parasite infection. If they are cleared, remove the infected dwarf hamster to an environment where it is on its own until the infection has been cleared.

Fleas
- on your dwarf hamster are clearly visible, just as they are on a cat or dog. Dwarf hamsters rarely get fleas because they do not go outside. If your dwarf hamster has fleas, they could have been transmitted by your other household pets, or if you have just acquired your dwarf hamster they were likely picked up from unhygienic conditions in the pet store or breeder. Fleas can make your dwarf hamster (and other pets) feel very uncomfortable because the flea bites itch constantly, so your dwarf hamster will be scratching itself constantly. Some dwarf hamsters (and other pets) have an allergy to flea bites and that can lead to very inflamed skin and hair loss. If fleas are not addressed quickly it can cause your dwarf hamster to become very sick. Fleas feed off blood, so an infestation of feeders will result in your dwarf hamster becoming anaemic which will cause its immune system to weaken and make it susceptible to any range of infections that its body will be too weak to fight off.

Fleas can be mistaken for mites by the untrained, so it is vital that you confirm that your dwarf hamster has fleas and not mites. The difference between the two different parasites is very obvious. Fleas are quite large and are very fast moving if you rub your finger against the fur growth of your dwarf hamster's coat. They will quickly move out of view, but what you will see between your dwarf hamster's fur are fine black faeces. If you put your dwarf hamster on a piece of white kitchen paper and dust some of these fine faeces on the paper and then wet them with a drop of water, you will see the paper turn red. That is because the faeces are comprised of your dwarf hamster's blood that they have been feeding off. Mites on the other hand are very small and barely visible to the naked eye, so if you rub your finger against the fur growth of your dwarf hamster's coat you will notice the skin is inflamed and flaky. Mites are covered separately in a later paragraph.

Once you have confirmed that your dwarf hamster definitely has a flea infestation, it is vital to check your other household pets. If your dwarf hamster is newly acquired, swift action is required to prevent the spread of fleas not only to other pets, but to your carpets and fabric furnishings. Fleas can jump quite far, and they will easily be able to move from your dwarf hamsters living environment in search of another host to feed off.

Because dwarf hamsters are so very small, it is advisable to consult your veterinarian for advice on buying products that are safe to use on your dwarf hamster. Regular flea killing sprays that are available at pet stores and retailers for cats and dogs can be very dangerous for a dwarf hamster because the chemical content can be too high for such a small animal to tolerate. Generally, the products will be in a spray or shampoo, but bear in mind that dwarf hamsters should never be bathed in water and get their coat wet, because that could strip their coat of vital oils. Your veterinarian will give you directions on how to use the products on your dwarf hamster and these must be followed to-the-tee to ensure that your dwarf hamster does not inhale, ingest or get toxins in its eyes.

You will also have to thoroughly treat your dwarf hamsters living environment to ensure that there is no re-infestation. Remove everything from the living environment and all substrate, nesting material, sand and food must be discarded and other items and well as the entire cage or tank must be thoroughly sprayed or washed down with a dwarf -hamster-safe flea killing product. Also treat the area directly outside your dwarf hamsters living environment in-case fleas have escaped the enclosure. Once you have thoroughly dried the living environment, you can replenish with new substrate, nesting material and food and return your dwarf hamster to its home. Keep a check over the next few weeks for any sign of re-infestation.

Mange
- or Sarcoptic mange, is a microscopic mite that infests the skin by burrowing in to embed themselves and feed off your dwarf hamster. Your dwarf hamster could have contracted an infestation from other household pets, or if you have recently acquired your dwarf hamster it could have been contracted from unhygienic conditions in the pet store or breeder. Another source of infestation can be from substrate or nesting material that is poorly packaged and purchased from pet stores that are unhygienic.

Scarcoptic mange is highly contagious and extreme hygiene, including wearing protective gloves, must be practised when handling your dwarf hamster if you suspect it has mange. Scaroptic mange can be very easily transmitted to other household pets and even humans. In humans it manifests as scabies.

Symptoms of a scarcoptic mange infestation will become visible very quickly. You will notice that your dwarf hamster has become very itchy and scratches constantly. The areas scratched will become inflamed and flaky, and there will be visible patches of hair-loss.

If you suspect scarcoptic mange, take your dwarf hamster to your veterinarian who will do a skin scarping and confirm an infestation by identification under a microscope. If your dwarf hamster is one of a pair or part of a community it is best to have them all checked because these parasites are highly contagious.

Your veterinarian will treat your dwarf hamster immediately with an injection and then give you medication in drop form to continue the treatment at home. Any dwarf hamsters that are diagnosed with scarcoptic mange must be isolated from all others and the living environment that they inhabited must be thoroughly disinfected. If there are other non-infected dwarf hamsters living in the same environment they must be moved out immediately.

All substrate, nesting material, sand and food must be discarded completely, and it is recommended that it be safely incinerated before throwing it in a bin because the parasites can survive for quite some time without a host. Disinfect the affected living environment as well as all accessories with strong antiseptic solution. Wear protective gloves and discard them once done. The living environment and accessories should be left open in a room where it will stand in direct sunlight and not be used again for a few weeks. Before introducing your dwarf hamster or hamsters to the living environment again it should be washed out and sanitised with a weak bleach dilution of 1 part bleach to 32 parts water to ensure that any parasite remains are removed.

Mites
- are extremely small parasites that attach themselves securely to the hair follicles of your dwarf hamster (and other pets). Viewed under a microscope, they have a scaly exterior that allows them to hook themselves to the skin of their host so that they can feed without becoming dislodged. If the infestation is not treated and your dwarf hamster is exposed to parasitic mites for a prolonged period of time

it can lead to sickness and skin disorders. Your dwarf hamster could have contracted an infestation from other household pets, or if you have recently acquired your dwarf hamster it could have been contracted from unhygienic conditions in the pet store or breeder.

Symptoms of mite infestation include inflammation around your dwarf hamster's ears, eyes and nose as well as scratching and rubbing against cage bars or other accessories. Initially there may be no other visible symptoms, but if you do notice the pre-mentioned symptoms, a trip to your vet is advisable because a long-term infestation can lead to more serious health complications.

If you suspect a mite infestation, place your dwarf hamster on a piece of white kitchen paper and gently comb its coat with a very fine toothed comb. Tap the comb on the paper and you should see the tiny parasites fall from the combs teeth. If you see the mites after combing, take your dwarf hamster to your veterinarian for treatment. If your dwarf hamster is one of a pair or part of a community it is best to have them all checked and treated. Your vet will recommend drops or a spray, or a combination of both. You can also get a spray that is especially produced for dwarf hamster safety that you can use to kill mites in their living environment after an infestation.

Any dwarf hamsters that are diagnosed with mites must be isolated from all others and the living environment that they inhabited must be thoroughly disinfected. If there are other non-infected dwarf hamsters living in the same environment, they must be moved out immediately.

All substrate, nesting material, sand and food must be discarded completely. Disinfect the affected living environment as well as all accessories with dwarf hamster safe mite killing spray or a strong antiseptic solution. The living environment and accessories should be left open in a room where it will stand in direct sunlight and not be used again for a few weeks. Before introducing your dwarf hamster or dwarf hamsters to the living environment again it should be washed out and sanitised with a weak bleach dilution of 1 part bleach to 32 parts water to ensure that any parasite remains are removed. Mites cannot be transmitted to humans.

Pinworms
- are not often diagnosed in dwarf hamsters, but they can occasionally become a host for small internal infestations of pinworms. Most dwarf hamsters diagnosed with pinworms would have contracted them from their breeding environment. Pinworms live in the dwarf hamster's large intestine and are not known to cause any distress or side effects to their host other than an itchy anus. If diagnosed by a veterinarian, it would most likely be by chance while treating the dwarf hamster for an unrelated condition.

Pinworms are easily treated with drops. If your dwarf hamster is one of a pair or lives in a community it is best that you have all treated for pinworm infestation because pinworms are easily transmitted via faeces.

On diagnosis of pinworm, all dwarf hamsters must be removed from their living environment immediately and it must be thoroughly disinfected. All substrate, nesting material, sand and food must be discarded completely. Disinfect the affected living environment as well as all accessories with a strong antiseptic solution. The living environment and accessories should be left open in a room where it will stand in direct sunlight and not be used again for a few days. Before introducing your dwarf hamster or hamsters to the living environment again it should be washed out and sanitised with a weak bleach dilution of 1 part bleach to 32 parts water to ensure that any parasite remains are removed.

Pinworms can also be easily transmitted to humans via faeces, but because they are not easily detected it is vital that you practice strict hygiene when cleaning your dwarf hamsters living environment and when handling and playing with your dwarf hamster. Wash your hands thoroughly before and after putting them into your dwarf hamsters living environment.

Tapeworms
- are the most common internal parasite contracted by dwarf hamsters. They live in the small intestine and your dwarf hamster could be host to a tapeworm for all of its life without ever experiencing any adverse symptoms. On occasion the tapeworm can cause an intestinal blockage, which could lead to serious complications for your dwarf hamster, including death. Symptoms to look for are loss of weight despite normal feeding and diarrhoea. If you suspect your dwarf hamster has a tapeworm infestation, take it to your veterinarian promptly because it can be very easily treated with drops to kill the parasite.

If your dwarf hamster is one of a pair or lives in a community, it is best that you have all of them treated for tapeworm infestation because tapeworms are easily transmitted via faeces.

On diagnosis of tapeworm, all dwarf hamsters must be removed from their living environment immediately and it must be thoroughly disinfected. All substrate, nesting material, sand and food must be discarded completely. Disinfect the affected living environment as well as all accessories with a strong antiseptic solution. The living environment and accessories should be left open in a room where it will stand in direct sunlight and not be used again for a few days. Before introducing your dwarf hamster or hamsters to the living environment again it should be washed out and sanitised with a weak bleach dilution of 1 part bleach to 32 parts water to ensure that any parasite remains are removed.

Tapeworms can also be easily transmitted to humans via faeces, but because they are not easily detected it is vital that you practice strict hygiene when cleaning your dwarf hamsters living environment and when handling and playing with your dwarf hamster. Wash your hands thoroughly before and after putting them into your dwarf hamsters living environment.

Reproductive System

- diseases occus in both female and male dwarf hamsters, but are most prolific in females who are bred over and over again. In the wild dwarf hamsters have a specific breeding season, but captive dwarf hamster have lost that instinct so many unscrupulous breeders will allow a female to produce back-to-back litters and this takes a toll on her health.

Female Reproductive Diseases

Birth Complications
- must be considered if your dwarf hamster fails to give birth within the expected time for her species. If your dwarf hamster is overdue giving birth to her pups you must take her to your veterinarian immediately who may administer medication to induce labour or decide to do a caesarean to deliver the pups.

Birth complications are a common problem with hybrids and unscrupulous breeding because often the female is too small to birth the pups she is carrying. In many cases the pups are stillborn. If the female is not provided medical assistance very soon after the date her pups are due, she too will die.

Mastitis
- is an infection of the mammary glands and occurs about a week after birthing pups. Your dwarf hamster's teats will be inflamed and swollen and can have a pussy discharge.

The pups must be removed immediately when the condition is identified because it will be painful for her to suckle them and some mothers will kill their pups.

You must take your dwarf hamster to a vet as soon as possible for antibiotic treatment.

Ovarian cysts
- are quite common in dwarf hamsters and are not life threatening. They can vary in size and can go undetected, rupturing on their own with you knowing. In short, a cyst is a sac of fluid that is considered harmless as long as they do not grow to a size where they begin to displace internal organs and tissue or hinder the dwarf hamster movement. If you suspect your dwarf hamster may have an ovarian cyst, it is best to take her to your veterinarian for treatment.

In general, ovarian cysts are benign and they do not spread nor increase the risk of cancer. Some dwarf hamsters have a genetic predisposition to ovarian cysts.

Pyometra
- is an infection of the womb and is a life threatening condition that can occur in breeding and non-breeding female dwarf hamsters. It can be caused by a bacterial infection or by hormonal changes in the uterus lining. It causes a build-up of blood and pus in the uterus. It can be found in females of all ages, but is more predominant in older females. It is believed that bacterial infections are introduced to the womb via the cervix. The disease presents in two manners, open pyometra and closed pyometra. Shared symptoms of both open and

closed pyometra include loss of appetite, increased water intake and urination and lethargy.

Open pyometra is easier to treat if picked up early and thus has a better prognosis. With open pyometra, the dwarf hamster's cervix is open and allows the blood and pus to drain from the uterus and leak out via the vulva. You will notice traces of blood and pus in your dwarf hamsters living environment. Dwarf hamsters don't menstruate, so any blood in a female's (and male's) living environment must be investigated.

Closed pyometra is a very serious condition with a much poorer prognosis, because the cervix is closed and the blood and puss cannot drain from the dwarf hamster's uterus, very quickly causing the abdomen to swell and become distended. Because a distended abdomen is often the first visible symptom, the infection is most often in an advanced stage and becomes very difficult to treat. Bacteria and other toxins can leak from the uterine walls into the bloodstream causing sepsis (blood poisoning). This can happen with both open and closed pyometra. If this happens it will cause other organs like the liver, kidneys and even the brain to begin shutting down. Your dwarf hamsters chances of survival even with treatment, is very small. Sepsis almost always results in death.

Male Reproductive Diseases

Penile plug
- can be fatal if it goes undetected or is left untreated. Your dwarf hamster's penile opening can become blocked and even infected. It is important that you regularly check your male's penis to ensure that it is not blocked because any blockage will prevent him from passing urine.

Initially there may be no symptoms and your dwarf hamster will still feed and remain active. If you are not cleaning out soiled substrate daily, you may not notice that your dwarf hamster is not urinating. First symptoms may include your dwarf hamster positioning himself to urinate, but passing no urine. He may also begin to squeak in pain. If it progresses, infection will set in and your dwarf hamster will become lethargic, stop feeding and could die.

Early detection of a penile plug can easily be treated by a veterinarian, leaving your dwarf hamster with no infection or other side-effects.

Testicular tumours
- are not uncommon in dwarf hamsters. Males have fairly large testicles and they are developed by no later than six weeks of age. Any change in the size and colour of the testicles must be monitored. If the testicles become permanently enlarged, swollen, inflamed or painful to the touch you must seek immediate medical care because it can be tumours. Even benign tumours can become malignant if left untreated. The only treatment for testicular tumours is castration.

Respiratory infections
- are one of the most common dwarf hamster ailments and they contract respiratory tract infections as easily as they do humans. Unlike humans though, these infections can affect dwarf hamsters far more seriously, very quickly escalating to pneumonia and death. Infections can be transmitted through exposure to other household pets as well as humans who are sick. Dwarf hamsters with a common cold or flu will present with typical symptoms including sneezing, mucous discharge of the nose and eyes, difficulty breathing, wheezing, rough feel and sound in the chest, inactivity, shivering and loss of appetite.

It is best to take your dwarf hamster to your veterinarian for treatment to prevent pneumonia or other complications. If you have other dwarf hamsters or pets, isolate the sick hamster until it has recovered to prevent transmission. Also practice strict personal hygiene for your sake and your hamster's.

As with humans, healthy dwarf hamsters are more likely to avoid contracting cold and flu and if they do, they will recover easier. Poorly cared for, sickly and older dwarf hamsters are more inclined to contract colds and flu, and also more likely to suffer complications or die.

Ringworm

- is a not a parasitic infestation, but a fungal infection that grows in your dwarf hamster's hair, nails and skin. As the fungus grows, the hair falls out leaving bald patches of skin on your dwarf hamster's body.

Ringworm is more inclined in plastic living environments that have poor ventilation and high humidity. Plastic is not a natural environment for any living creature and should be avoided.

Your veterinarian will be able to confirm a diagnosis of ringworm and provide medication to treat the condition. Treatment is both topical and internal and generally lasts for a minimum of four weeks to rid the dwarf hamster's body of the fungus. If your dwarf hamster is one of a pair or part of a community, it is best that they all be checked by the veterinarian, even if there are no visible symptoms of ringworm. If only one dwarf hamster is affected, it must be isolated until treatment is complete and the condition has cleared up.

Your dwarf hamsters living environment must be thoroughly disinfected and if the living environment is made of plastic, thoroughly disinfect it and throw it out for recycling. Provide your dwarf hamster with a kinder, more ethical home.

Ringworm is a highly contagious fungus and extreme hygiene, including wearing protective gloves, must be practised when handling your dwarf hamster if you suspect it has ringworm. It can be very easily transmitted to other household pets and even humans.

All substrate, nesting material, sand and food must be discarded completely, and it is recommended that it be safely incinerated before throwing it in a bin because the fungus can be very persistent. Disinfect the affected living environment as well as all accessories with strong antiseptic solution. Wear protective gloves and discard them once done. The living environment and accessories should be left open in a room where it will stand in direct sunlight and not be used again for a few weeks. Before introducing your dwarf hamster or hamsters to the living environment again it should be washed out and sanitised with a weak bleach dilution of 1 part bleach to 32 parts water to ensure that any parasite remains are removed.

Strokes
- in dwarf hamsters often occur overnight. The first symptom you may notice is that your dwarf hamster's gait is unbalanced and its head is tilted to one side. Strokes most often occur in older dwarf hamsters, but can occur in younger dwarf hamsters as well, especially if they are exposed to excessive heat.

Other symptoms of a stroke include running in circles and bouts of trance-like staring. Some dwarf hamsters may need help with drinking and feeding. There is no cure for damage done to the body by a stroke, but over time some mobility issues and other conditions can heal themselves, as in humans.

If your dwarf hamster suffered a mild stroke, it can recover and the effects will wear off over time. The prognosis of a severe stroke must rest on veterinary advice, but the future quality of life of your dwarf hamster must be paramount when making any decision.

Teeth

- are vital to a dwarf hamster's survival so it is important that you keep your dwarf hamsters diet as close to their natural diet as possible, avoiding processed foods like sugar, chocolate, peanut butter, bread, etc. Apart from damaging your dwarf hamster's teeth, these food items can become compacted in its cheek pouches leading to infection and even starvation.

Dental Cavities
- form when your dwarf hamster is being fed a diet high in simple carbohydrates. Treats containing sugar like honey, chocolate, etc should be avoided; even seeds coated in sugars should be avoided. Cavities can cause teeth to rot and can also cause the formation of abscesses which can make your dwarf hamster very sick.

Symptoms include excess salivation, weight loss, and swelling of the mouth or face. Cavities/caries need veterinary attention, which will include antibiotic treatment and possibly the extraction of the tooth.

Malocclusion
- occurs when your dwarf hamster's teeth are not worn down sufficiently, causing them to overgrow and prevent your dwarf hamster from eating.

Like all rodents, dwarf hamsters have one pair of incisors and three pairs of molars in their upper and lower jaws. There is a sizeable gap between the incisors and the molars, separating incisors for gnawing and molars for chewing. Dwarf hamsters have open-rooted teeth that grow continuously throughout their lives. In the wild, hamsters feed on very hard foods and also grind their teeth down by gnawing on wood and other hard plant materials. It is vital that you provide your captive dwarf hamster with sufficient healthy hard materials to ensure that its teeth remain at a healthy length.

Malocclusion results if you fail to provide sufficient hard chews for your dwarf hamster. Constant chewing at cage bars is a sure sign that your dwarf hamster does not have enough healthy chews and chewing at the cage bars will not solve the problem, it will only cause further harm to your dwarf hamster's mouth and teeth. Your dwarf hamster may also not be able to adequately gnaw its teeth down due a misalignment in the upper and lower jaws that could have been caused by external trauma such as an injury, constantly chewing at metal cage bars or was present at birth due to genetics.

Symptoms of malocclusion include decreased appetite, weight loss, swelling of the mouth or face and excessive salivation. If you think your dwarf hamster has malocclusion, it must be taken to your veterinarian to have its teeth clipped. Clipping the teeth yourself is strongly discouraged because without the right equipment your dwarf hamster's teeth can shatter. Dwarf hamsters rely on strong healthy teeth for their survival.

Dwarf hamsters fed on a healthy diet and provided with a healthy variety of chews should not develop over-grown teeth. If your dwarf hamster has a birth defect that causes its teeth to overgrow, you may need to have its teeth clipped weekly to keep it healthy.

Wedged
- food bits or chews can also cause abscesses in your dwarf hamster's mouth if they become lodged for a period of time. Excessive salivation and weight loss are the obvious symptoms. It is best to take your dwarf hamster to the veterinarian to ensure that all bits of wedged material are removed and your dwarf hamster is

treated with antibiotics. It is not recommended that you remove materials lodged in your dwarf hamsters teeth because if the smallness of your dwarf hamsters mouth and because it should be done with the proper tool to prevent injury or breaking a tooth.

Tumours

- are an abnormal growth of cells in an area of tissue or an organ. The growth can be benign or malignant. Benign tumours are not cancerous and do not spread; these are the most common tumours found in dwarf hamsters. Malignant or cancerous tumours that spread from one area of the body to another are very rare in dwarf hamsters, being diagnosed in less than 5% of tumours.

In dwarf hamsters, tumours can occur throughout the body, including the adrenal gland, lymph glands and nodes, spleen, liver, womb, intestines, brain and skin. Tumours are more common in older animals and tumours in the womb and mammary glands are more common in females used for breeding. The sooner the condition is diagnosed and treated by a veterinarian, the greater the chance of a positive prognosis.

Symptoms of a tumour will depend on the location of the tumour. Topical tumours are clearly visible and often present as a bulge together with hair loss and inflammation on the skin. Internal tumours may present with loss of appetite, lethargy, depression, dullness of the eyes and coat, diarrhoea (sometimes with blood content) and abdominal pain. All of these symptoms must be taken seriously once you become aware of them and you need to take your dwarf hamster to a veterinarian for diagnosis without delay.

Internal tumours will be identified by ultrasound or x-ray, and a tissue sample will then be extracted for biopsy to establish if the tumour is benign or malignant. Surgical removal will be the most likely outcome to prevent the tumour from increasing in mass or spreading to other areas of the body. Surgical removal of tumours in the early stages definitely improved the chances of a full recovery, but late detection does cause some tumours to become malignant (cancerous), in which case the prognosis is very poor for such a small little animal.

The cause of tumours can be genetic or environmental, and the exact cause it very difficult.

If your dwarf hamster does undergo surgery to remove a tumour you must ensure that it does not groom the operation wound, as this will interfere with the healing process. Also follow all medical advice given by your veterinarian with regards to cleaning and dressing the wound until it is healed.

Urinary Tract
- infections and complications are many in dwarf hamsters, just as in humans. The urinary tract comprises of the kidneys, ureters and bladder. Infections can affect any area of the urinary tract, or the whole urinary tract.

Bladder
- can include bacterial infections (cystitis), corrosion, crystals, polyps, stones and tumours. There are are all common and serious conditions that your dwarf hamster could suffer from and all need veterinary treatment. Bladder conditions have similar symptoms, but don't try diagnosing the condition yourself because any time delay in proper treatment could prove fatal for your dwarf hamster.

Symptoms of bladder disease can include increased water intake, loss of appetite, lethargy, loss of condition, increased urination, no urination at all, bad smelling urine, bloody urine or distended abdomen. If you see any of these symptoms, changes in behaviour and changes in appearance of urination and frequency of urination –

take your dwarf hamster to a veterinarian. A urine sample, ultrasound or x-ray will be necessary to confirm the diagnosis and appropriate treatment. Your dwarf hamster could need antibiotic treatment or even surgery. Bladder disease is a serious condition and must not be ignored.

Ask your veterinarian what the potential cause is of bladder infections, crystals or stones, if any of those are the diagnosis, to see if you can introduce preventative measures to your dwarf hamster's diet or water quality.

If your dwarf hamster does undergo surgery to remove polyps, tumours or stones you must ensure that it does not groom the operation wound as this will interfere with the healing process. Also follow all medical advice given by your veterinarian with regards cleaning and dressing the wound until it is healed.

Kidney

- disease or renal failure, commonly affects older dwarf hamsters, although it can be diagnosed in younger dwarf hamsters that have diabetes. Symptoms include increased water intake and increased urination. You may notice traces of blood in the urine. If your veterinarian diagnoses renal failure you will be advised that there is no treatment for renal failure in dwarf hamsters.

Wet-Tail

- is a common disease in Syrian hamsters. Dwarf hamsters are not susceptible to wet tail, but many dwarf hamster human parents will often misdiagnose any diarrhoea as wet-tail. Although it is highly unlikely to be the diagnosis, it is still recommended that any dwarf hamster with diarrhoea be taken to your veterinarian.

Death and Euthanasia

If your dwarf hamster has an incurable condition or injury that compromises its quality of life or causes constant pain, it is vital to put the interests of your dwarf hamster before your own emotions. Pain is pain, whether experienced by an animal or a human being. Ask yourself how it would be for you to experience what your dwarf hamster is experiencing. Remember too that as human beings we can take a vast array of medications to alleviate pain and suffering. We can even take medication to relieve stress and trauma. Medication for dwarf hamsters in very limited and they too can suffer from stress and trauma as well as depression.

Many pet lovers form a genuine bond with their pets and come to love them, viewing their pet as part of their family. If your veterinarian has given you a very poor prognosis on your dwarf hamster's condition, ask questions about its quality of life. Ask too if having your dwarf hamster humanely put to sleep would be a kinder decision than allowing it to suffer.

Think it over carefully and if necessary, discuss it with your family. If your vet has recommended euthanasia, then the most loving decision would be to gently put an end to your dwarf hamsters suffering. If your dwarf hamster is part of a human family with children, gently explain your decision to them. You may have feelings of guilt, but if your decision was made with love then those feelings of guilt will pass. It is quite normal to experience feelings of loss when we lose a beloved pet. Allow your feelings and those of your children if you have to take their natural course until they pass and you can remember your little dwarf hamster with joy again.

Chapter 9: Breeding Dwarf Hamsters

Since this book has been written for small animal lovers who want to educate themselves on dwarf hamsters in captivity as pets and how to care for them, breeding will not be covered in depth as breeding dwarf hamsters (and any other pet) is strongly advised against.

Breeding should be left to those with expert knowledge who are willing to invest time and money in the care and health of the animals that they are breeding.

The aspects of breeding covered in this chapter are purely for novice dwarf hamster human parents who have inadvertently, and through no fault of their own, found themselves with a female dwarf hamster in gestation. Dwarf hamsters breed at a very young age, they breed easily and regularly in captivity so you may have acquired a new female dwarf hamster without knowing that she has conceived.

Many people breed domestic pets so that their children can see the miracle of life first hand. This is irresponsible pet ownership and immature parenting! There are more than enough books and television programs that can teach your children about the miracle of life. What you are in-fact teaching your children is that pets are owned like possessions to be used and abused at the pet owner's behest, without any consideration for the pet's future and in the case of breeding, for the future of the off-spring. Responsible parenting will teach children that we do not own pets like possessions, but rather we assume responsibility for their future life by taking good care of them, including their needs in our daily routine and loving them as an extension of our family.

There are other people who think that they can make money by breeding pets and selling them. That is an uninformed decision! There is little money to be made from breeding any pets, including dwarf hamsters. Commercial en-masse breeders are constantly flooding the market with new pups and pet stores are generally over-stocked.

Breeding dwarf hamsters without any in-depth knowledge is irresponsible and can cause suffering to the female if she encounters any birthing problems and can cause suffering and abuse to the pups if they are just given away to anyone who will take them. Many people take on pets that they do not know how to care for, and it is always the pet that ends up paying a horrible price for human ignorance and negligence.

Do not buy dwarf hamsters with the intention of breeding them for a reason! If you are an expert breeder you would not be reading this book.

Female versus Male Genitalia

If you are looking to buy a pair of dwarf hamsters it is vital that you are able to know what sex each of them is before bringing them home. In most species, a pair of young females can happily co-exist and bond, so two females is your best option. Although two young males can co-exist, the risk of territorial fighting can definitely become a problem in the future, especially if the living environment does not allow enough living space for each to move freely in his own territory. Hybrid breeding has also led to dwarf hamster temperament being less predictable, so you could experience fighting at a later stage among two females as well.

Dwarf hamsters can live very happily on their own and adjust very well to a solitary life as long as their living environment provides plenty of variety and stimulation, and you give your dwarf hamster daily attention.

If you acquire a female and a male, you will definitely end up with a litter of pups and that you definitely don't want, so buying from an experienced seller is vital. Many pet store assistants do not have the knowledge required to sex dwarf hamsters, even though they may claim they have. Buying online or from classified adverts is just as unreliable when it comes to the sex of the dwarf hamster you order. If you buy from an ethical breeder you should be fine as they generally care very much about the animals they breed, but some study beforehand won't do you any harm.

Sexing Dwarf Hamsters
Your first challenge will be to position the dwarf hamster in your hand so that you can carefully scrutinize its underbelly. Considering the small size, the fact that your scent is unfamiliar and the dwarf hamster had possibly had limited human contact - you could find yourself holding a wriggling little fur-ball that refuses to cooperate with you. It is best to have someone assist you by gently cupping the dwarf hamster in their hand, keeping a finger gently under its head, and gently restraining kicking limbs with their thumb and other fingers. This will allow you to look very carefully.

It is very difficult to sex dwarf hamsters under three weeks old because they have not yet reached sexual maturity. The most obvious difference at this age is the space between penis and the anus versus the space between the vagina and the anus. There will be an obvious space between the penis and the anus, and in an adult dwarf hamster that space can be up to one centimetre or one third of an inch. The space between the vagina and the anus is fractional, and the two could appear to be a single vent. Another difference is that only female dwarf hamsters have nipples. If you run your finger gently along its underbelly you may feel the four pairs of nipples running along either side of her abdomen.

In older dwarf hamsters it is slightly easier because the genitalia have matured. You may, however, have more of a challenge turning the dwarf hamster over to look, so if it cannot be held down, try placing it in a small glass container with a flat bottom so that you can view the underbelly that way.

Once the genitalia have matured the space between the male penis and anus and female vagina and anus is more noticeable. The males' tail area will also appear elongated because the scrotum has developed. Nipples on females will be more pronounced.

Caring for a Female in Gestation and After Birthing

Male dwarf hamsters can reach sexual maturity from four weeks and females from as early as five weeks. It is not ethical to breed a five week old female, but many pet stores do not separate the sexes and you do risk unintentionally buying a young female in gestation. You may not be aware of her condition until she is very close to birthing. The gestation period of dwarf hamsters is between eighteen and twenty two days, depending on the species.

If this does happen, you have a responsibility to take care of your female dwarf hamster and her pups. The moment you willingly chose to acquire her you made a commitment to take care of her health and welfare. She is fully dependent on you for survival!

Initial signs that your female dwarf hamster is in a gestation period will only become obvious in the week before birthing. You will notice an enlarged abdomen and nipples. If you have acquired her as one of a pair of females, remove the other female; you can try re-introducing them once the pups have been removed, but it is not guaranteed that they will happily co-exist again. If you inadvertently bought a male and female pair, remove the male and keep them permanently separated because you do not want any more pups!

Try not to disturb the female in gestation or pick her up, as this could cause her stress. Replace substrate, nesting material, food and water while keeping your distance. Speak softly to her to reassure her. In that way she stays accustomed to your scent and voice. As birthing comes closer, your female will begin to build a nest in a place in the living environment where she feels safe. She may begin to eat slightly more, and will hoard more food in her nest. It is vital that you do not physically touch her at this stage, or try to feel the babies because this will cause extreme stress, and in some instances females will abandon or cannibalise new born pups if she feels that the environment is threatening and unsafe.

Ensure that you are feeding her the very best food that you can afford in the days before birthing, but don't make dramatic changes to her diet because you don't want to upset her stomach and potentially bring on a bout of diarrhoea. Additional protein like nuts, small bits of hard-boiled egg or oats can be included in her diet, but only in very small amounts.

In the days immediately preceding birthing, keep her in a quiet environment with limited outside movement or sound. During this time she will continue preparing her nest, and at the onset of labour she can appear quite frantic, alternating between eating, nesting and grooming. At this time she can become openly aggressive, so keep your distance and allow her space. She will give birth in her nest to anywhere between six to twelve pups, but if she is very young the litter will most likely be small.

If your dwarf hamster has not given birth despite showing signs of imminent birthing, you must watch her very carefully. If you notice discharge and blood leaking from her vulva she may be experiencing birth problems and need veterinary assistance. She may also begin squeaking loudly from pain. Labour can be induced, and your vet may be able to assist in removing pups from the birth canal. If the first pup is still born, it can cause problems for the remaining pups because they literally become stuck behind the dead pup blocking the birth canal. Without veterinary assistance, the remaining pups will die and ultimately the female will die a very agonising death as well. Some veterinarians will perform a caesarean to assist your dwarf hamster in giving birth to her pups, but not all veterinarians will take the risk. Remember, dwarf hamsters are very small little animals and the pups are tiny. Trauma of surgery could kill the mother and her pups. In extreme cases there may be nothing that can be done to assist the mother with birthing and you will lose the mother and the whole litter. This is more common in females bred too quickly, hybrid breeds and indiscriminate breeding, as this could happen in a pet store where females and males of all ages are kept together.

Even if your female successfully gives birth to a litter of pups that are her first litter and she is too young, she may reject them or begin to cannibalise them. It is only in this instance that you must intervene and remove the mother from the enclosure to save the pups. The mother may have become very aggressive, so a receptacle is best used to lift her from the living environment. Gently remove the pups, keeping them in their nest and keep them in a separate enclosure. Care of the pups must be your first priority as they are very vulnerable. Caring for rejected pups will be covered in a later paragraph. Once you have dealt with the pups, remove and replace all the substrate and remaining nesting material and place the mother back into the living environment without the pups. Give her time to relax and become calm. There are many factors that could have caused her to instinctively behave in the manner that she did towards her pups. Conceiving when she herself was still a pup could be a very strong factor. Be gentle with her and give her time to recover.

If all has gone well with the birth and the mother is clearly nursing and taking care of her pups, do not interfere with them at all for the next two weeks. Female dwarf hamsters recognise their pups by scent so if you handle the pups and put your scent on them, the mother could reject or attack them.

Continue to change the food and water while keeping your distance, but don't clean the substrate or nesting material. Speak softly to the mother, as you always have done, to reassure her. After about seven to ten days you will start seeing the pups becoming active and begin to venture from their nest. Do not make any attempt to touch them or pick them up because they are still very dependent on their mother and she will still be very protective of them. At this time you can begin to put small amounts of food in the enclosure for the pups to introduce them to solids. You can use standard dwarf hamster pellets soaked in water. At first the pups may ignore the food, but keep putting fresh soaked pellets in their enclosure and they will begin to feed when they are ready.

Once the pups are out and about in the enclosure and begin feeding on solids it is vital that you ensure that they have access to clean drinking water as well. Check if they can reach the spout of the water bottle and if not, lower the water bottle to bring it within their reach.

At this stage you can begin to handle the pups without the mother becoming protective towards them. By three weeks of age the pups should be feeding well on solids and nursing less. Their appearance will be just like an adult dwarf hamster, just a bit smaller. At four weeks, male pups must be removed from the living environment, and the female pups should be removed by no later than five weeks. Keep male and female pups separate because males can reach sexual maturity at four weeks and females at five weeks. You definitely don't want to be responsible for another litter of pups!

Caring for Abandoned Pups

If your female dwarf hamster is going to abandon or cannibalise her pups, it will be within the first few days of birth and can often happen immediately after birth.

As a novice dwarf hamster human parent this poses a massive problem because taking care of such tiny babies that are totally helpless, deaf, blind and hairless requires skill and experience.

Once you are aware that the mother has rejected her pups, remove her immediately from the living environment and separate her from the pups so that she does not cause them any harm. Gently remove the pups, keeping them in their nest and keep them in a separate enclosure. Care of the pups must be your first priority as they are very vulnerable. Keep them covered and do not expose them to open air or handle them more than necessary. Very small pups can easily succumb to hypothermia so they must be kept warm all the time. The easiest solution is to put hot (not boiling water) into a water bottle or even a drinking bottle and wrap a towel around it. Ensure that the heat emitted is warm and not hot. Place the towel wrapped bottle in a cardboard box and level it out if necessary by covering it with substrate. Gently place the nest with the baby dwarf hamsters in on-top of the substrate and loosely cover the box to keep heat in, but still allow for ventilation.

If you bought the mother from a breeder, contact the breeder no matter what time of day or day of the week. These pups have been placed in a life-or death situation and time is of the essence if they are to survive. If you did not buy the mother from a breeder, contact your veterinarian without delay. Call them on their emergency number if it is afterhours. Tell them that you have abandoned dwarf hamster pups that need to be taken care of. Your veterinarian will either put you in touch with a breeder or ask you to bring the pups in without delay. The pups can be hand raised and fed formula specific for dwarf hamster pups, but this must be undertaken by people with expert experience. Breeders would be best to do this as the pups would need to be housed in special incubators and fed and stimulated, as they would be by their mother.

The ideal would be to find a dwarf hamster that has just birthed a litter and introduce the pups to her for her to foster. Again, it would only be a breeder that would have healthy breeding females who might foster the pups. If it is a big litter of pups that has been rejected, a breeder can introduce them to more than one lactating female. Dwarf hamsters can be accepted and raised by Syrian hamster females as well. Either way, without in-depth expertise you must not try to raise the pups yourself because they are very fragile, they require around-the-clock care and specialised formula that may not be readily available.

Chapter 10: Further Online Reading

There are many informative websites and interactive online groups where you can research and find information about dwarf hamsters. Most websites and groups include Syrian Hamsters (much larger and the most common hamster kept as pets) and Chinese Dwarf Hamsters, both of which are not included in this book because they are of a different genus and thus not dwarf hamsters.

Highly informative and recommended websites include:

Hamsterrific.com – "Where hamsters would surf the net ... if they could use a computer."

Hamsterific.com offers a broad range of information on hamsters, from taming to sexing to heath care and breeding as well as everything in-between. The site is easy to read, easy to navigate and includes beautiful pictures of hamsters as well as wonderful videos.

Hamsterhideout.com – "Fun & informative hideout for hamster lovers."

Hamsterhideout.com is a quirky looking site that at first glance seems irrelevant and sparse, but once you begin clicking on the links it has loads of valuable information to offer!

There are contributions from readers and the contributions range from poetry to academic papers. Definitely do pop in to this site to see if it suites your style.

AAAhamsters.org – Linda Price's Hamstery

AAAHamsters.org is a site concerned with the breeding of hamsters for good temperament and show qualities.

Although breeding should not be the interest of novice human dwarf hamster parents, this site does give you insight to ethical breeding standards as opposed to en-masse "anything goes" breeding standards.

Well worth a visit for some insight on ethics and caring about the quality of dwarf hamster pups produced.

DwarfHamsterblog.com – Dwarf Hamster Blog. The Dwarf Hamster Guide by Sarah.

DwarfHamsterblog.com is an entertaining and informative site for dwarf hamster enthusiasts. It is full of interesting, valuable and some fun information as well as pictures and submissions by readers.

Another site that should definitely be bookmarked if you are serious about caring for your dwarf hamster!

Hamsters-uk.org –is the site of the National Hamster Council in the United Kingdom.

Hamster-uk.org is a hive of information for serious hamster human parents. Apart from selection and care, it also includes information on showing hamsters professionally as well as show dates.

It also gives you details on who to contact to find registered breeders as well as details about hamster clubs

If you live in the United Kingdom and you are considering getting serious about your dwarf hamster's care and good looks, visit this site for information!

Afrma.org – is the site of the American Rat & Fancy Mouse Association.

Afrma.org includes dwarf hamsters. It provides valuable information on selection and care as well as list of registered breeders, information on showing hamsters professionally and show dates.

If you live in the United States of America and you are considering getting serious about your dwarf hamster's care and good looks, visit this site for information!

Copyright and Trademarks: This publication is Copyrighted 2017 by Zoodoo Publishing. All products, publications, software and services mentioned and recommended in this publication are protected by trademarks. In such instance, all trademarks & copyright belong to the respective owners. All rights reserved. No part of this book may be reproduced or transferred in any form or by any means, graphic, electronic, or mechanical, including photocopying, recording, taping, or by any information storage retrieval system, without the written permission of the authors. Pictures used in this book are either royalty free pictures bought from stock-photo websites or have the source mentioned underneath the picture.

Disclaimer and Legal Notice: This product is not legal or medical advice and should not be interpreted in that manner. You need to do your own due-diligence to determine if the content of this product is right for you. The author and the affiliates of this product are not liable for any damages or losses associated with the content in this product. While every attempt has been made to verify the information shared in this publication, neither the author nor the affiliates assume any responsibility for errors, omissions or contrary interpretation of the subject matter herein. Any perceived slights to any specific person(s) or organization(s) are purely unintentional. We have no control over the nature, content and availability of the web sites listed in this book. The inclusion of any web site links does not necessarily imply a recommendation or endorse the views expressed within them. Zoodoo Publishing takes no responsibility for, and will not be liable for, the websites being temporarily unavailable or being removed from the Internet. The accuracy and completeness of information provided herein and opinions stated herein are not guaranteed or warranted to produce any particular results, and the advice and strategies, contained herein may not be suitable for every individual. The author shall not be liable for any loss incurred as a consequence of the use and application, directly or indirectly, of any information presented in this work. This publication is designed to provide information in regards to the subject matter covered. The information included in this book has been compiled to give an overview of the subject s and detail some of the symptoms, treatments etc. that are available to people with this condition. It is not intended to give medical advice. For a firm diagnosis of your condition, and for a treatment plan suitable for you, you should consult your doctor or consultant. The writer of this book and the publisher are not responsible for any damages or negative consequences following any of the treatments or methods highlighted in this book. Website links are for informational purposes and should not be seen as a personal endorsement; the same applies to the products detailed in this book. The reader should also be aware that although the web links included were correct at the time of writing, they may become out of date in the future.

CPSIA information can be obtained
at www.ICGtesting.com
Printed in the USA
BVHW052142120623
665866BV00019B/318